W9-BDL-523

TURNING POINTS:

How The Salvation Army Found a Different Path

ALLEN SATTERLEE

© 2004 by The Salvation Army

Published by Crest Books, Salvation Army National Headquarters
615 Slaters Lane, Alexandria, Virginia 22314
(703) 299–5558 Fax: (703) 684–5539
http://www.salvationarmyusa.org

Printed in the United States of America

All rights reserved. No part of this publication may be reproduced, stored in a retrieval system, or transmitted in any form or by any means—electronic, mechanical, photocopy, recording—without the prior written permission of the publisher. Only exceptions are brief quotations in printed reviews.

Book design by Laura Ezzell

Library of Congress Control Number: 2004112589

ISBN: 0-9740940-3-X

Scripture taken from the Holy Bible, New International Version.
Copyright 1973, 1978, 1984 by International Bible Society. All rights reserved.

Table of Contents

Foreword v

Preface vii

TURNING POINT ONE: The Role of Women 1

TURNING POINT TWO: From Conference to Command 13

TURNING POINT THREE: Thy Blood–Washed Army 23

TURNING POINTS FOUR: Internationalism 35

TURNING POINTS FIVE: The Sacraments 45

TURNING POINT SIX: *In Darkest England* 59

TURNING POINT SEVEN: The First World War 71

TURNING POINT EIGHT: The First High Council 81

TURNING POINT NINE: World War II and Its Aftermath 97

TURNING POINT TEN: Renewal 111

Endnotes 120

Bibliography 127

Foreword

How does one try to get his mind around a movement like The Salvation Army? It is a church, but without the traditional sacraments. It has a military-style government, but a mission of compassion. It seeks social reformation, but spiritual redemption is its first priority. It came into existence at a time of urban hopelessness, but it developed a practical plan for the rehabilitation of urban ghettoes that was redolent with optimism. It emerged in a world of male domination, but defied the sexist culture of Victorian Christianity by opening opportunity and leadership to woman. It has eschewed party politics, but worked for laws that protect the most vulnerable.

It is unified internationally under one General and government system, but its methodologies around the world are as varied as the nationalities and cultures of its members. It is small in size for an international denomination (closer to one than two million members), but its influence far exceeds its numbers. All its local units (corps) have the same basic mission, but individual corps vary considerably in constituency and ministry.

How does one explain this Salvation Army?

Allen Satterlee has tackled the challenge, and he has done so in an extremely helpful way. He has selected ten watershed events and decisions that either set the Army on a course or constituted a crucial course change. He recognizes that there were other happenings that helped to shape the organization, but he believes that his ten were the most decisive. Few could argue with his selection.

With The Salvation Army, we have what Satterlee likens to the platypus, a creature absolutely unique, unlike any other. Implicit in this book is a rejection of any attempt to make the Army more like other churches or any other respected institution. It is what it is, and that uniqueness is its gift. Times bring about change. The shifting missional terrain requires constant adaptation. But what The Salvation Army essentially is—a church for the excluded, an army of salvation, a mission of compassion, a people hungry for holiness, and a community renewed—should never change.

We can thank Allen Satterlee for helping us understand.

Commissioner Philip D. Needham
September 2004

Preface

Never in the history of the world has there been an organization like The Salvation Army. When the Founder, William Booth, decided to combine the existing ecclesiastical structure of the Christian Mission with the ancient framework of the military it was more than a gimmick. Something new was created. If that were not enough, in 1890 he plunged the Army into a full frontal attack on society's ills. The organization further mutated with the incorporation of the social service ministry. When this happened a religious denomination also became a social service agency. To this day there is nothing else quite like it.

Salvationists are often concerned about the confusion of their identity. "They don't know we're a church!" they say. For some this creates a constant sense of angst. They want to blend in with their Christian brethren but find their uniforms won't allow it. For these, the Army's uniqueness is more a bit of embarrassment than anything else. "If we could just tone it down and try to get in step with the rest of Christendom," they cry plaintively. Most officers who have attended ministerial associations will know even their enlightened colleagues in ministry are not quite sure how to regard these who have traded in "Reverend" for "Captain."

Not only that, but those who represent the Army in the social service realm will know that their colleagues are not sure how to take them either. Their desire to compartmentalize an individual into parts rather than treat a person as a unit is contrary to The Salvation Army's focus on the whole person, as necessary, for any permanent solution to be possible. Sometimes regarded as less than professional, Army folk may be treated with bemused tolerance.

The public as a whole either doesn't understand or doesn't care who the Army thinks they are. The general sense is that they don't comprehend all the slogans and ranks and bands and open-airs and the like. But they like The Salvation Army because it seems to be doing something consistently right, something that makes sense at the heart level. So when they hear the band playing its carols or see the little lady by her kettle stand at Christmas, there is the spontaneous tribute of coins, a vote of confidence for the Army to keep on doing what it is doing.

So what are we to conclude? We would like to think of ourselves as a lion, an eagle, a bear or some other noble creature. In reality we are most like the platypus, that creature that defies classification because it is neither mammal nor fowl. It has fur and appears mostly mammal. But then there are those webbed feet and the eggs it lays. The platypus is not too terribly bothered by the problems we humans have in classifying it. It simply is what it is.

We in The Salvation Army need to quit wringing our hands about what is different about us and rejoice that God has allowed us our own distinct identity. People don't know we're a church? What a great opportunity to witness when we tell them. The social services folks don't understand our motivation? What a great chance to share with them our understanding of Christian compassion.

Because we have this freedom we are free to try things that others dare not. There is freedom in being different. Just ask the platypus.

The chapters that follow outline key moments in the history of The Salvation Army. They share certain characteristics in common.

1) Each one had a decisive affect on the character of the Army.

2) Each directly influenced and continues to influence every generation following.

3) Each represents God's continued interest and faithfulness to the Army.

The author freely admits that there are other important events in the Army's history. The opinions are his own based on his study. Other opinions are expected. The author encourages dissenters to research and present their own.

As for this book, I am deeply indebted to a number of people for their kind assistance. My wife, Esther, took the reins at the corps when I was away doing research, patiently listened to my excited explanations of things I cared about which she found of little interest, proofread the manuscript and constantly encouraged me.

Major Omer McKinney, an avid student of history, provided comments and suggestions that were very helpful in improving the manuscript. Major Frank Duracher also assisted with smoothing out a number of rough spots. In Singapore, Commissioner Lim Ah Ang provided helpful suggestions. His stature as a Salvation Army leader in Asia commands respect.

The International Heritage Centre in London provided invaluable materials and assistance. The same is true for The Salvation Army National Archives and Research Center in Alexandria, Virginia, USA. The staffs at both went beyond the call of duty to answer my questions and to seek answers for me.

The people of my corps appointment in Bradenton, Florida have always been wonderful. They were very supportive during the time I wrote this book. When I was away doing research they were particularly helpful to my wife as she carried extra duties, making the seven years in this appointment the happiest we have ever had.

I would also like to thank my administrative assistant, Judy Thompson. When she took this job, she had no idea she would be shipping books, manuscripts or making frequent trips to the post office for overseas mail. She has done this with grace and constant efficiency.

I would like to thank my divisional commander of the Florida Division, Lt. Colonel Donald S. Faulkner. My involvement in this project has taken me out of my appointment a number of times. He has not only allowed me this opportunity but always supported me in pursuing this project. Although I deeply respect him as my superior, I more deeply value him as a friend.

Finally, this book was completed while serving in our first overseas appointment in the Singapore, Malaysia and Myanmar Command. The kind assistance and support of the Lieut–Colonels David and Grace Bringans, Officer Commanding and the Command President of Women's Ministries are also deeply appreciated.

The Role of Women

"I want to say a word." That simple statement challenged the Christian world and set the development of The Salvation Army. It occurred in an English church away from the spotlight and years before any thought of The Salvation Army existed.

During a childhood of poor health, Catherine Mumford became an avid reader, especially of the Bible and religious literature. The strength that might have defined a youthful body was instead directed to her mind and spirit. She formed opinions—very strong opinions—about what was right and wrong. These included an abhorrence of alcohol, a heartfelt desire for personal holiness and, of greatest historical importance, the equality of women in ministry. When she met young William Booth she found one who lacked her reticence to speak, whose physical energy contrasted her bodily frailty and whose fervent love for the Lord matched her own. He saw in her the gentleness of character that balanced his crudeness; a wonderfully developed mind that filled in the gaps for his broad-stroke thinking and one whose strength made her more appealing than the traditionally submissive women of the Victorian era. Through a long and lovely courtship Catherine influenced William more than he influenced her. His wisdom was best demonstrated by listening.

One of the issues that revealed their unique understanding and temperament was the equality of women. Booth held the common view of his day that, compared to a man, a "woman has a fiber more in her heart and a cell less in her brain."[1] It is not surprising that he felt that way. Women in nineteenth–century Britain and in the rest of the world were denied the right to vote. Education readily available to boys was routinely denied to girls. No woman had ever occupied a seat in Parliament or distinguished herself in the fields of science, religion or education. A woman was defined, not by her own abilities but by her relationship with the males in her life—as a daughter, sister, wife or mother. It was from this identification with the dominant males in her life that she was to derive her satisfaction.[2] As someone has written, "Home is the divinely appointed sphere, affording abundant scope for the energies of woman."[3] It was neither unusual nor uncharitable for William Booth to expect this from his future wife. Of course, this was before he encountered Catherine Mumford who had little respect for the status quo.

W. T. Stead described Catherine's belief "that the progress of the human race as a whole was seriously retarded by the hateful doctrine which in every age has persistently depressed fifty percent of its number below the recognized human level."[4]

In light of the logical but loving reasoning of Catherine, William reexamined his views. From doubt to tolerance and then to full support he progressed, until he was an advocate of woman as man's equal. Though this was a victory for Catherine it would not be enough. One couple might have this question settled but there was still a world that regarded women as the eternal second class. She could see it when she went to the market or when she talked with friends. But when she heard it from the pulpit it was intolerable.

Stepping Forward

Her first battle came early on. While attending a neighboring congregational church, the newly converted Catherine heard the gifted minister Dr. David Thomas make a derogatory remark about women. Although embarrassed at her own boldness and intimidated by Thomas' professional stature, she could not be restrained. Writing to him, she voiced her disappointment.

> In your discourse on Sunday morning . . . your remarks appeared to imply that doctrine of woman's intellectual and even moral inferiority to man. . . . Permit me, my dear sir, to ask whether you have ever made the subject of woman's equality as a *being*, the matter of calm investigation and thought? If not, I would, with all deference, suggest it as a subject worth the exercise of your brain.[5]

Although nothing seems to have resulted from this, it forced Catherine to develop her thoughts. It prepared her well for the clash that would come after she married William. Despite her calls for equality, their marriage had by her choice become a traditional nineteenth century marriage. As a minister's wife she assumed the role narrowly defined by Church custom: someone to be seen but largely silent. It was this reality of her life which conflicted with the conviction of her soul that nagged at her. It took an attack on another woman to awaken her.

Dr. Walter Palmer and his wife Phoebe were touring England. While there they created quite a stir because *both* Dr. and Mrs. Palmer preached. The idea of a woman preaching was considered by many to be scandalous. A certain Dr. Johnson spoke for many when he said, "Sir, a woman's preaching is like a dog's walking on his hinder legs. It is not done well, but you are surprised to find it done at all."[6] Anglican minister Arthur Augustus Rees was so incensed by women preaching that he wrote a pamphlet denouncing the practice. Reading his attack, Catherine had seen and heard enough. It was now time to go public.[7]

Her response, originally titled *Female Teaching* but eventually renamed *Female Ministry,* not only answered Rees' objections but further outlined the biblical standard of a ministry that was neither male nor female. She argued,

> If the dignity of our Lord or His message were likely to be imperiled by committing this sacred trust to a woman, He who was guarded by legions of angels could have commanded another messenger; but, as if intent on doing her honor and rewarding her unwavering fidelity, He reveals Himself *first* to her; and, as evidence that He had taken out of the way the curse under which she had so long groaned, nailing it to His cross, He makes her who had been first in the transgression, first also in the glorious knowledge of complete redemption.[8]

And she would take up additional arguments:

> The first and most common objection urged against the public exercises of women is that they are unnatural and unfeminine. Many labor under the very great but common mistake of confounding nature with custom. Use, or custom, makes things appear to us natural which in reality are very unnatural, while on the other hand novelty and rarity make very natural things appear strange and contrary to nature. So universally has this power of custom been felt and admitted that it has given birth to the saying "second nature."[9]

But Catherine found that even writing the pamphlet was not enough. While defending a woman's right to preach successfully, she remained silent. Her own retiring nature filled her so full of dread that she would not, could not speak. The conflict in her soul increased. Finally on Whit Sunday, 1860, at their Methodist Church in Gateshead, Catherine surprised herself, her husband, and the large congregation present. As William was ending the service, Catherine spoke to her husband barely above a whisper, "I want to say a word." She then testified about her spiritual struggle, knowing she ought to speak but not doing so.

> I daresay many of you have been looking upon me as a very devoted woman, and one who has been living faithfully to God, but I have come to know that I have been living in disobedience . . . but I promised the Lord three or four months ago, and I dare not disobey.[10]

When she sat down, William seized the moment to commend her for taking the step he had so often urged her to take. "My wife will bring the message tonight," he announced.

Salvation Army pioneer George Scott Railton, with a somewhat less refined argument than Catherine Booth might espouse, said:

> What *is* women's work if not to preach? The devil made her the first preacher on earth, and the result of her first sermon was the ruin of us all. And now she must not preach anymore! Of course not! Devil!—how clever a deceiver you are.
>
> Woman's first wrong step was looking too much after food, and too little after divine things, and the devil and the churches he has so largely mastered would fain point woman in the same direction still. "Cook! Cook! Cook! Oh, noble woman, behold the object of thine existence!"
>
> Woman of God, make thy choice! There is the stage—the open–air stand. The multitudes will crowd to hear thee—no matter what thy name, thy position, thy abilities—simply because thou art woman. If thou, by the power of God, no matter whether with finished oratory, or with faltering, disconnected phrases, shalt move their hearts, they will come, and come again, and thou wilt see many of them fall at the feet of Jesus, if thou will but go forth and speak to them.[11]

As an example to her sisters in the faith, Catherine rose to that challenge by not only continuing to speak but also becoming one of the outstanding female preachers of her day. It was her example that began to win over the opposition. Not only was she preaching but she was far superior to many of the male preachers of her day. Thousands crowded her meetings while the press often reported her sermons verbatim. She challenged her critics by saying, "Before such a sphere is pronounced unnatural it must be proved that woman has not the ability to teach or preach, or that the possession and exercise of this ability unnaturalizes her in other respects."[12]

Making Equality Work

The natural progression from the pulpit was to infiltrate the operation of the organization itself. But this seems to have been more than Catherine Booth intended. Her son, Bramwell Booth wrote, "The Army Mother had never quite contemplated placing women in positions which would involve *their authority over men.* This would be going further than anything recorded in the early Church. The Founder delayed for a considerable time before making the decision."[13] Nevertheless, as the Christian Mission was formed, the position of women became one of the early defining distinctions of the new movement. For the first time in Church history, the role of women in ministry was outlined as integral to mission. The Constitution of the Christian Mission boldly stated:

> Section XII *Female Preachers*—As is manifest from the Scripture of the Old and New Testaments that God has sanctioned the labors of Godly women in His Church; Godly women possessing the necessary gifts and qualifications, shall be employed as preachers itinerant or otherwise and class leaders and as such will have appointments given to them on the preacher's plan; and they shall be eligible for any office, and to speak and vote at all official meetings.

The impact of women was immediately apparent in the growing Mission. In 1878, forty–one of the ninety–one evangelists in the field were women. With a sense of gratification, William Booth wrote, "In externals nothing is more remarkable in the recent progress of the Mission than the great advance of our female ministry. It has sometimes been said that female preachers would be the ruin of the Mission. But on the contrary, it turns out that the prosperity of the work in every respect just appears most preciously [precisely?] at the very times when female preachers are being allowed the fullest opportunity."[14]

When the Christian Mission later changed its name and became The Salvation Army, the resulting explosion of growth would have been impossible without women officers. An example of the impact of women was seen in 1890 when William Booth plunged the Army fully into the field of social work. He could never have given thought to the plan had he been restricted to men officers. In the United States, women pioneered more corps than married couples and single men combined. Not only did women make a mark on The Salvation Army, in a very real sense they *made* The Salvation Army.

Opposition

This did not come without opposition. Upsetting the established order of things is seldom observed quietly. Reverend P. Prescott, one of the many British clergy who viciously opposed The Salvation Army, included a salvo for women preachers:

> It is that honorable shame, that sensitive delicacy, that shrinks from whatever is improper and impure, which the Creator has implanted in the female mind and as the guard and defense of her virtue. When that defense is destroyed, female virtue is not destroyed but it has become like a city without walls. And I put it to every sensible man and woman, whether Nature itself does not teach us, that for a woman to address a congregation of men is not the surest way to destroy that shamefastness which is the guard of female virtue?[15]

Few of the attacks against this aspect of Army work were so delicately worded. Typical of the day, a more scathing attack is to be found in the *Birmingham* (Alabama) *Age Herald:*

> We have just found out that (there are) some members who are wonderfully strengthened in their religious faith . . . by seeing a woman beat the tambourine over her head, while a lot of trifling men were tooting brass horns and gyrating to the music of "Possum up a gum stump, Raccoon in the Hollow." . . . If it's proper for young ladies to parade in the

streets, enter saloons and dives, and herd together without regard to sex . . . in what they call "barracks," then the Salvation Army is entitled to the respect and support of good people; but if womanly modesty and safety, as well as common decency, is required in religious matters, then they are not entitled to that respect. . . . We have a good deal of sympathy for these poor girls, who have been induced to leave their homes and roam about the country in hope of serving God to better advantage in the Salvation Army; and, just before a daughter of ours starts out on such a religious jaunt as this, we will send her to the insane asylum, where she can be properly cared for and treated for mental indigestion.[16]

Opposition came not only from outside the movement but from within. The culture had bred a man to believe that, as lowly a position as he might occupy, he was still superior to a woman. Raised in a society that accepted with little question the brutal treatment of women by men, the converted were willing to accept that abuse of this nature was no longer to be tolerated. But accepting orders from a woman was unacceptable to some men. Some resigned rather than accept this. Others struggled tremendously.

Women's Impact on the Movement

Despite opposition, the role of women continued to increase within the Army. After Catherine Booth's death in 1890, the fact of women's participation became integral to The Salvation Army. Later the Founder would write to his soldiers concerning the contributions of women.

I am sure you will agree with me as to the value of the salvation heroism she has displayed in the past years of our history. She has descended into the foulest slums of the great cities. She has sought out and rescued the most helpless of her own sex. She has fought and conquered the roughest, coarsest and wildest of men. She has presented a holy example to the most ignorant and savage tribes of the heathen by living amongst them. She has nursed the sick and blessed the dying; and, following the example of her Lord, has laid down her life in her efforts to deliver others from destruction.

On the other hand, her ministrations have found access to

the hearts, and a welcome to the homes, of the richest and highest of almost every land where our Flag is flying. She has filled with honor the most important positions of authority in our ranks, and directed with success many of our difficult enterprises.

Indeed, she has justified every demand ever made by the Army upon her capacity, her courage and her love.

Woman has done well for The Salvation Army.[17]

Has it worked? From the standpoint of serving the Army's needs, the truth of Booth's statement is evident. Women have continued to influence the Army in every sphere. The office of the General has twice been occupied by a woman. Women officers continue to give key leadership throughout the Army world. In every territory, command and region married and single women outnumber men in the ranks. While other conservative Christian denominations have wrestled, or continue to wrestle, with the issue, female leadership has been an established principle for the Army. Though many cultures continue to keep women in subservient roles, Army women have had astonishing success as they have fulfilled their responsibilities, earning respect where it was unnatural to have it.

Remaining Challenges

A number of problems remain nevertheless. The leadership of The Salvation Army remains dominated by men. Many women come to the Army married or soon marry other officers, and their service is merged with that of their husband. The conservative nature of the Army continues to look largely to the male officer over the female when an appointment is made. The married woman officer's role tends to be more narrowly defined than the male married officer's role. While many married women officers assert that their ministry is never limited, it is because they have actively sought a ministry rather than having it clearly outlined for her, as it is for her husband.

The International Commission on Officership in 2000 voiced these concerns felt by many women, saying, "A number of women officers experience frustration and lack of fulfillment, perceiving that they are not considered for certain appointments due to gender or marital status." The commission suggested that "territories affirm the ministry of women officers by appointing them to positions commensurate with their gifts and experience." It further recommended that "territories seek a gender balance in the membership of planning and decision–making bodies."[18] Even this deserves further exploration. In all the varied cultures where the Army serves, there are some constants. One of these is that it is universally accepted that when children enter the family, the mother will be the primary caregiver. This means that when children interrupt the days, as they invariably do, it is accepted that the mother will be the one who will most likely attend to these needs. If a call from headquarters is made to an appointment, it is found to be far more acceptable if the mother is at home tending to the sick child than to find that the father is. This is often by mutual agreement between the parents. However, the result is that a woman's opportunity to develop her leadership is limited accordingly.

Another factor limiting women from fully occupying roles that they might assume is the restriction placed on a woman's development because of stereotyping. This is as likely to occur in the corps with local officers as it is in the ranks of officers. While local officer positions are shared between the sexes, gender domination still exists among specific positions. Most corps sergeant–majors are male; most young people's sergeant–majors are female. It is far more common to find a woman songster leader than a woman bandmaster. It is safe to say that a woman is offered more opportunities than she would find in almost any other Christian denomination. This does not change the fact that these roles can still be restricted. As Major Wanda Browning states, "While today's confident married woman officer is often allowed to speak with love and tact, she sometimes discovers that her robust personality must be kept in check as she offers her leadership indirectly."[19]

Women also have not always been given the opportunity to explore their leadership skills in the same way that men traditionally have been given. It is not reasonable to expect a woman to serve as a divisional commander if she has not been allowed to develop her administrative skills along the way. Some may possess natural gifts, but even these need to be developed. Commissioner Flora Larsson, in her book *My Best Men Are Women,* quotes Salvation Army officer Laura Petri: "It is more difficult for women to reach the high positions than men. To be advanced, a man requires hardly more than average gifts. A woman must be superior."[20] That this has been a challenge since the early days is evidenced by

William Booth's plea, "All I ask—let us find out the powers of our women comrades, whether they belong to our own families or not, and give them the chance to use those powers for the glory of God and for the salvation of the world."[21]

Interestingly, a woman's access to leadership positions in Western countries has been largely *more* restricted than in non–Western countries. It is not unusual to find a woman in a leadership position as a reinforcement officer in a developing country, but she might find herself frozen out of similar leadership positions in her homeland. On the other hand, some women have often been reluctant to take advantage of opportunities when they have been offered, perhaps out of complacency or a sense that they lack ability. Again, this is not a new problem. Catherine Bramwell–Booth wrote, "It seems to me many women are called to fill a place of high authority, called by the world's need as well as by God and the Army, but few are chosen *because few have fitted themselves*."[22] Even earlier the Founder, William Booth, wrote, "Woman must do more for herself. She has not always done all she might have done to maintain the position given her, and effectively discharge the duties connected with it."[23]

Present Realities

At one time the Army's stance on women marked a bold, new approach to ministry. But since that time the world has caught up and what was ground breaking is now accepted practice in most of the world. Since the Army first ordained women and placed them in positions of authority, women have almost universally gained the right to vote and with that occupied high public office as well. Women are now regularly found in corporate boardrooms and are increasingly made heads of large corporations. Although a few denominations still fail to recognize women's ordination, most do give them access to some ministry functions. The Army proved that women could handle leadership and ministry in all phases of its work. Now it may find itself passed by, viewed as being mired in tradition instead of as a tradition–breaker.

While in many parts of the world women's roles have been elevated, it is not true everywhere. This is particularly true of countries with majority Muslim populations. Although The Salvation Army does not operate in many Muslim countries, Pakistan and Indonesia have very active Army operations. Both of these countries, however, are vying for leadership in the Muslim world. The trend toward Islamic fundamentalism in these nations can represent a particular threat to the Army on several fronts.

Extreme Muslim fundamentalism insists on a prescribed role for women, one very much at odds with the Army view. The Taliban insurgents of Afghanistan proved how far this can go. Under their regime, women were banned from walking with anyone other than their husbands in public, were not allowed to appear without their faces covered, and were barred from holding jobs or attending school. Although this has not happened yet in any Muslim country where the Army operates, should such extreme Islamic influences reach these countries where the Army now operates, Salvationists might find themselves especially targeted for their stand on women. Our women officers and soldiers could very well become victims of intolerance.

Regardless of the difficulties, a woman's opportunity to excel survives within The Salvation Army. In fact, the Army could not exist without the woman officer. In many places, the corps could not function without the female local officers. Indeed, in far too many places the corps is dominated by women—not because they wish it so, but because the men have forsaken it. The Salvation Army owes to women a debt beyond measure. Despite misgivings about their place or whether they are fully appreciated, the women of the Army continue to render invaluable service to God and His kingdom.

All of this because in an otherwise unremarkable moment in time, one woman stepped forward and said, "I want to say a word."

From Conference to Command

Without any famous names or planned campaigns, the Revival of 1859 burned its way from its birthplace in Wales and spread to England's heart. Marked by fervent prayer, it spread primarily among the working classes. Largely opposed or disdainfully ignored by the ordained clergy and mainline denominations, large numbers of people were converted and the saints quickened. Often without denominational support for their newfound evangelistic zeal, lay workers and new converts formed independent associations to reach England for Christ. One of these, the East London Special Services Committee, found that there was no richer field for soul–winning than Mile End Waste. It was to this group that the itinerant preacher William Booth applied for work. Although his application was filed, no action took place to engage him despite his impressive record of revival work.

In July 1865 William Booth came again in contact with the East London Special Services Committee. After a meeting and a walk through Mile End Waste, he came home and proclaimed to his wife, "I have found my destiny!"[1] The group enlisted him to conduct meetings in a tent erected on an unused portion of a Quaker burial ground. Meanwhile street meetings were conducted in front of The Blind Beggar pub. The work met with great success, and it didn't take long for Booth to ascend to the position of leader.

Booth appears to have ended his association with the East London Special Services Committee on friendly terms, and he soon formed his own group to handle the growing movement. Booth's new "Conference" conferred on organizational matters and decided issues by a majority vote. At first, Booth was not opposed to this arrangement. He recalled later, "Under the idea that teaching my brethren law–making would increase their sense of responsibility and unite us more fully together, I launched the Conference on a sea of legislation."[2] Any charms that this system seemed to offer soon evaporated. Members became absorbed in the process, vetoing each other, making, amending, passing and tabling motions, each member vying for the opportunity to plan the Mission to their desired end. Robert Sandall records, "the energies of the older missioners were absorbed by committees—they had become committee–men rather than active workers."[3]

For the work of God to advance as it should, Booth might have been best advised to adjust to the vagaries of democracy. Instead, the work was bogged down. Soul–winning became an afterthought. The crisis was reached in 1876 when the Mission recorded only 200 new members added for the year. "It was little wonder that new members were not coming forward. They had to face a variety of committees to test the depth of their conviction and to see their progress after a set period. Committees had to be consulted if members wanted to exhort or give out tracts or aid in social work. Committees and discussions were of over–exaggerated importance and it seems clear that preachers were recording converts who soon became backsliders, possibly because of the bewildering array of interviewing groups."[4]

Beyond this, Booth found that when there was an opportunity to advance, he needed the freedom to take the initiative. Waiting for the Conference to meet, discuss plans, amend or table them, question and discuss them further seemed to Booth a foolish waste of time. Action needed to be taken, and there was no time for this endless process. More and more he acted without the Conference's approval, deciding instead to report to them what he had done rather than seek their permission. In spite of this, the Conference continued to meet. George Scott Railton notes, "As each Conference came round, it became more and more evident to everyone that what was done or not done during the year had little to do with any resolution of the Conference."[5]

Change Initiated

This did not escape the notice of others in the Mission. Three early leaders, George Scott Railton, William Ridsdel and Bramwell Booth, approached Booth. "We gave up our lives to work under you and those you should appoint, rather than under one another." Ridsdel stated. "You tell us what to do and we'll do it. I can't see the good of a lot of talk, with one wanting one thing and another another."[6]

Already some measure of power had been given to Booth in 1870. The amended Conference rules stated that the Superintendent shall "possess the power of confirming or setting aside the decisions and resolutions of any of the official, society, or other meetings held throughout the Mission, which in his judgment may be in any way prejudicial to the object for which the Mission was first established." Also given to Booth was the office of Superintendent for life and the right to appoint his successor. In 1875 he further solidified his control when he obtained the right to override any actions of the Conference. Finally in 1878, after the meeting with Ridsdel, Railton, and his son Bramwell, Booth was prepared to take the boldest step of all.

Booth called the thirty–two evangelists who composed the 1878 Conference and outlined how the future would look. Democracy would not work for the Mission. It was too slow and cumbersome. They were committed to obeying Booth anyway. It was time to decide for him, for themselves, for the Mission and, as Booth asserted with prophetic authority, for the kingdom of God. To make certain there was no misunderstanding he flatly declared, "This is a question of confidence between you and me, and if you can't trust me it is no use for us to attempt to work together. Confidence in God and me are absolutely indispensable both now and ever afterwards."[7] Whether shell–shocked, overwhelmed by Booth's supporters or fully convinced of the logic of all this we cannot know, but when the vote was taken, the decision was unanimous for this change of leadership. The membership of record voted itself out of the right to ever vote again. Those dissenting are unknown, although history tells us a number left rather than accept the proposed form of government.

The daring of this move by Booth was amazing. Conversely, Great Britain joined the rest of the Western world as it moved away from the concepts of royalty and autocracy in favor of democracy and socialism. Labor unions were rapidly forming, asserting the rights of the individual workers over factory owners. Marxism was born at the same time with its tenets of power invested in the people. Even church denominations were placing more power in the hands of its people, partly because they were following the flow of events and partly as a result of demands from its membership. That Booth took his organization in an entirely different direction flew in the face of all conventional wisdom. It emphasized leadership authority over the individual, an almost foreign concept in nineteenth century Britain.

A Protestant Pope

Sometimes it appears from Salvation Army history that William Booth possessed a mystical charismatic quality that led his troops to follow him. Although there certainly were those who were blindly loyal, Booth had the opposite effect on most who met him. He was dismissed as a clown, derided as a heretic, demonized as a cult–like leader, attacked viciously from the pulpit, the Parliament and the press. Over the years, thousands would join the Army but thousands also left because they found they could not abide the way it operated. Some would write their own attacks and supposed exposés of the Army's inner workings, and regale a scandal-hungry public with tales of how false the Army was from top to bottom. In his later years Booth may have been widely respected, but in the early years he was regarded as a dangerous despot, an egomaniac who pursued power and sought personal gain above all else.

The change in the Army's government to an autocratic form brought about some of the most vicious attacks against Booth. One former officer claimed that in this system an officer was "henceforth a slave,"[8] while another writer claimed, "the Salvation Army government is the antithesis of freedom."[9] Still another wrote, "Through historic ages, no government, church, sect or society ever placed more power and supremacy in the hands than has this gentleman arrogated to himself in The Salvation Army."[10] Playing upon the strongly anti–Catholic sentiment that was widespread in Britain at this time, well–known clergyman Reverend P. Prescott complained, "If Mr. Booth had studied the New Testament as diligently as he appears to have copied the Constitutions of the Jesuits, we should not have had the Protestant Jesuitism that has risen up among us, in complete antagonism both to the Scriptures and to the genius of the English Constitution. This despotism may endure for a while, all power and all property being concentrated in one man. No difference of opinion is allowed; thus the despotism is extended, as far as possible, to the very thoughts; for when the expression of opinion contrary to that of the ruling power is not permitted, opinion itself becomes stunted and dwarfed."[11] Not content to attack the General, the author concluded that people as "patently ignorant as Salvationists seemed to be were probably best guided by someone who thought for them."[12]

Salvationists themselves were willing to acknowledge that the General carried authority out of proportion to the rest of the world. A 1916 editorial stated, "It is very difficult, if not impossible, to find a parallel position of influence to that occupied by the General of The Salvation Army. Certainly, no modern captain of industry comes anywhere near him for direct influence on his fellow–creatures."[13] In explaining the advantages of this position, Booth himself wrote:

> Such a combination or oneness of action will only be possible with oneness [of] direction. If all are to act together all must act on one plan and, therefore, all must act under one head.
>
> Is it not an axiom everywhere accepted, in times of war, at least, and we are speaking of times of war, that one bad general is preferable to two good ones? If you will keep the unity of 5,000, one mind must lead and direct them. Is this direction of one mind all the direction needed? By no means. Subordinate leadership there must be in all manner of directions; all the talent in this direction possessed by the 5,000 must be called into play, but one controlling, directing will must be acknowledged, accepted, and implicitly followed, if you are to keep the unity of 5,000 and make the most of it for God and man . . .
>
> Let every man fight as he is led, or every regiment charge up the hill and storm the redoubt or so any other deadly, murderous deeds according as they are resolved upon after discussion, and votes and majorities, and where will you be? What sort of telegrams will you send home to an expectant country, and what sort of welcome back will those of you that are left receive? No! obedience is the word. Somebody knowing what they are doing, to DIRECT, and then simple, unquestioning obedience.
>
> And then you must have discipline, order. Those who keep the commandments and who excel in service must be rewarded, and those who are disobedient must be degraded, punished, expelled.[14]

In large part the autocracy of William Booth worked because he was by nature autocratic. In personality he is reminiscent of the great military field commanders who combined information with intuition. Such individuals must have the freedom to move quickly, to seize opportunities when they are presented, to retreat when necessary, to promote and dismiss those who help and hinder along the way. Although Booth was human enough to smart when criticisms were fairly or unfairly leveled against him, he was remarkably single minded, pushing onward and forward to his goal. The wonder of his rule of the Army was never more clearly demonstrated than in 1890 when he had the whole Army close ranks and charge to enter the battle against social evil with the *Darkest England* scheme. (See Chapter 6.)

People reacted to his leadership in different ways. There were those who served for a time in the Movement but then chose to leave. Included in this number were such notable Christian leaders as Gypsy Smith and H. A. Ironside. There were those who were bitter and some who arrayed themselves as enemies of the Army. In a later bestseller, *Built to Last,* James C. Collins and Jerry L. Porras discuss successful businesses and the key leadership involved in visionary companies. They note, "Only those who 'fit' extremely well with the core ideology and demanding standards of a visionary will find it a great place to work. . . . Visionary companies are so clear about what they stand for and what they're trying to achieve that they simply don't have room for those unwilling or unable to fit their exacting standards."[15]

Almost a century and a half earlier Booth instinctively accepted that the polarizing effect the Army had on people was no reason to move it away from what he believed was his God–appointed task to lead and rule The Salvation Army. If there was any doubt as to his full conviction on this matter, it was cleared up later by members of his own family. The Booth children all followed their parents into the work and served as officers. But family connections did not spare the children from Army discipline. Choosing the integrity of the Army system over family ties, Booth forever lost three of his children to the Army when they would not conform to its demands.

While many could not function in the Army atmosphere, there were many who did. People from all walks of life came and offered themselves for service. Although the mission of the Army spoke to them, there was also the appeal of order. It seemed to many that if spiritual war was to be conducted, it must be waged under battle conditions. A clear command structure seemed an answer to this. For some the need was more fundamental. Conceived in chaos and raised in homes marked by turmoil, the

Army represented a place of order and security. Though the demands could be arduous, the expectations were clear.

Booth also had a keen way of recognizing talent and potential. Pedigree and refinement meant little to him—he knew little of that himself. What mattered was what he saw in the hearts of the young lassies, the newly converted drunkard, or the occasional minister who wandered into the Army. The early Army was built as much by these as by Booth himself. Although he was the unquestioned leader, he managed to bring together a remarkable team of people in top leadership to move the Army forward. Their loyalty to Booth was given freely and freely received. The autocratic Booth needed to have the full confidence that those under him would trust his instinct as being God inspired. And if for some reason he had misunderstood the divine direction, these subordinates would find their own relationship with God strong enough to make the General's plan work.

It was this system headed by the Founder that very soon made it possible for the Christian Mission to transition into The Salvation Army. The notion of The Salvation Army would have been impossible without it. Proof of this would come with two organizations formed in the United States which at first copied and then tinkered with the command structure. Both would become something, but not an army.

Change—Not Necessarily Improvement

In 1884, Thomas Moore was in charge of The Salvation Army forces in the United States. After some legal difficulties revolving around the organization's standing in the United States, he asked Booth for permission to incorporate The Salvation Army. Booth insisted that the Army in the States remain as it was in Britain with Booth as the title holder of all properties, in spite of the fact that United States law would not allow this. Incorporation would have solved the problem, but Booth insisted that property held in his name was the Army way, and Moore was to bring The Salvation Army in the United States into line. It would seem that either the Founder did not care what the United States law was or he distrusted Moore's information. (In fact, Moore was right. Later the Army was incorporated in the United States in 1898.) As the discussions escalated, Booth dispatched auditors to check Moore's books and to communicate the General's feelings. Although Moore was sound in his reasoning for incorporation, his books were in great disorder. After receiving the auditors' report back in London, the General issued farewell orders for Moore to proceed to South Africa.

Moore was incensed. He incorporated The Salvation Army and soon after proclaimed himself General of the newly named body—The Salvation Army of America. Booth dispatched Frank Smith to rally the remnants of the loyal forces, less than one–eighth of its former strength. The two Armies competed with each other for a time, but eventually Moore's poor administrative skills caused a split within his shrinking forces. These in turn split again, with one faction under Commissioner Richard Holz reuniting with the international Army in 1889.

What happened over the next seven years is still unclear. A group calling itself the American Salvation Army operated for a time and then dissolved. In 1896 the American Salvation Army was reborn under the leadership of James Duffin. The new Army copied the international Army in nearly every detail, causing considerable confusion for the public. This led then National Commander Evangeline Booth to bring legal action against the American Salvation Army. In 1910 the international Army won out and the American Salvation Army was banned from using "salvation," "army," the name of the Army's official publication "The War Cry," the use of blue uniforms and bonnets, or any term or form that imitated The Salvation Army. They subsequently changed their name to the American Rescue Workers.

The American Rescue Workers still exist in the northeastern United States. Their centers are called corps and their officers hold ranks. However, some time ago they gave field officers autonomy in their locations, allowing them to decide whether or not they would move when appointments needed to be made. The result has been a decline in the Rescue Workers. Corps are required to have only one meeting a week which can be held at any time. When the Commander–in–Chief needs to move someone to a new opening, the officer he calls can refuse with impunity. The Commander–in–Chief (there is more than one general) is elected. The past two commanders have decided to move the national headquarters to their city rather than to move to Philadelphia, the official national headquarters. At present the Rescue Workers number around twenty corps.

Another organization, the Volunteers of America, formed as a result of departures from the autocratic mold of The Salvation Army. This organization was founded in 1896 when the second son of the Founder,

Ballington Booth, resigned from his appointment as National Commander. A series of misunderstandings and grievances had arisen over a number of issues including the autocracy of his General father, and the Ballington Booths were issued farewell orders with no destination. First, the Ballington Booths said they would accept the orders, then refused them, but vowed not to form a rival organization. However, within days of their resignation they announced they were forming God's American Volunteers, soon renamed the Volunteers of America, a quasi–military organization very similar to The Salvation Army. The relationships between the organizations were officially respectful but unofficially contentious.

One of the most prominent differences was that the officers would elect the General of the Volunteers. This election process remains to the present day, but the organization itself has changed dramatically. Ballington Booth served as General until his death, after which his wife Maud was elected. There followed a series of generals with lesser ability than the Booths, and the organization languished. A radical change came in the 1980s when the Volunteers of America changed from a command structure to local boards of directors, retired their gray uniforms and eliminated ranks. The national CEO coordinates but does not command. The organization now holds one religious service a year to keep its desired church status. Although Volunteers of America directors are ordained by the organization, they are encouraged to attend any church of their choice.

The Volunteers abandoned their evangelistic religious roots as the democratic process ensued. Without clear direction the Volunteers of America lost their original vision and mission. A successful social service organization with complex and varied social programs, it has ceased to be an agency for the salvation of souls.

Strengths and Weaknesses of Command Structure

The Salvation Army's clear chain of command is one of its strengths. It is easily understood at the corps level and at headquarters. It also provides accountability. Although critics complained about Booth's unrestrained power, it was later demonstrated that even the office of the General is accountable (see Chapter 8). The command structure is also helpful in providing clarity of purpose and direction, as the individual in the Army benefits from the wider experience of many rather than relying on his or her own limited knowledge.

The command structure also keeps the Army focused on its overall mission and purpose. Operating in over one hundred countries amid a wide range of cultures, the Army could easily find itself drifting from its purpose in a less defined structure. It may be that the command structure's most important function over the years has been its ability to communicate effectively the Army's core mission and purpose. The two organizations cited earlier show that the tendency to drift from the original purpose is a constant hazard. Definition and direction must constantly be reinforced so that the Army does not fall into the trap of assuming that movement in any direction is the same as progress.

However, the command structure is not without its weaknesses. Its emphases on obedience and conformity could lead to promoting managers over leaders. This includes the threat that some in positions of authority might feel from those who "color outside the line" or who in other ways challenge presumptions held by the organization. It is doubtful that the Founder could work within the structure he created for others.

There is also the danger that those in command can become isolated. This is a danger at all levels from local officer to top leadership. Called "Group think," this has led to tragic results for nations and organizations. The Army is no less vulnerable. The Army's traditional sensitivity and overreaction to criticism from within and outside only add to this danger. The challenge is to stay in touch and relate to the larger world while continuing rigorous self–examination. An encouraging development has been the friendlier climate of more public debate about issues affecting Salvationists at all levels. Evidence has been seen in more frank discussion of issues affecting Salvationists in print in such magazines as *Salvationist* (United Kingdom) and *Pipeline* (Australia). International Headquarters has also invited public discussion through its website on a wide range of topics. Other actions, such as the International Spiritual Life Commission and the Commission on Officership, have also been helpful. This has not always been comfortable, as strong opinions elicit strong emotions. But it must be remembered that the early Church sharpened its understanding of the gospel truth because of the defenses it had to mount against the heresies that attacked it.

Although the command structure can seem at one point to be a warm coat and the next a straightjacket, had the Army not experienced this early turning point, it might never have been more than another obscure mission that lived a brief life, a historical footnote of Victorian England.

Thy Blood–Washed Army

In the waning days of the nineteenth century Great Britain stood as a supreme military power creating the *Pax Britannica,* the peace of Britain. Every citizen of the Empire was aware of the presence, prestige and power of the British military. Officer were members of the aristocracy, eager to make a name for themselves and find relief from boredom. The commoner found the military to be an answer to joblessness and a chance to travel to the ends of the earth. The uniform of their country offered all classes their identification with greatness. Coming home in that uniform provided opportunities to prove that whatever a man's roots, he could improve himself.

Christianity was enjoying its finest day since evangelizing the Roman Empire. A revival of experiential religion promised not only eternal life but a framework of joy and blessing to the new believer. There was talk that Christ's coming might be imminent as conversions were dramatic and plentiful. It was the age of the Palmers, Finney, Spurgeon, Moody, and Sankey whose meetings attracted thousands. The mood gave rise to songs of a military nature. Immediate hits included "Hold the Fort" and "Onward Christian Soldiers." Christianity was on the march, and the world was to be conquered.

Militancy in the Movement

Just prior to the nineteenth century, militancy described in the fledgling Christian Mission spurred the missioners to fight harder. They were beginning to use military terms and analogies because nothing else seemed to better fit what they were doing. Point man for the Mission's militancy was the fiery Elijah Cadman. Stationed in Whitby, England in 1877, he seized upon the visit of William Booth to make a billboard–sized poster. It called for 2,000 men and women to join the "Hallelujah Army," announced the visit of "general" William Booth, and was signed by "captain" Elijah Cadman (a title the locals had been using already for Cadman). Embarrassed at his own boldness, he hid the poster before Booth arrived. It was too late. Tipped off, the Founder commanded that the poster be produced. The nervous Cadman was relieved beyond measure when Booth expressed his delighted approval.

Others were commonly referring to Booth as general, a shortened version of general superintendent. It came then as little surprise that even as he was addressing the Christian Mission Conference on its need to abandon democracy in favor of his one man autocracy, William Booth told his followers that the military system was the best method for saving souls.[1]

The story concerning the actual name change is legendary. While working in 1878 on a proof piece for the Christian Mission, William Booth, his son Bramwell and George Scott Railton discussed its headline that read, "The Christian Mission is a Volunteer Army." The militia, termed "volunteers," were notorious for their low–level functioning and non–military bearing. Bramwell remarked, "Now see here! I'm a regular or nothing!" The Founder reflected for a moment, crossed the room and with pen in hand marked through the copy. The new banner read, "The Christian Mission is a Salvation Army."

Harold Begbie, official biographer of the Founder, reports that Booth considered the change to be of little significance.[2] This small notice also was reflected in "Salvation Army" being omitted from the 1878 Deed Poll, the legal document that established the organization. If anything, it was a subtitle to better explain what the Christian Mission was rather than meant to be a change in name.[3] Although it failed to register in the official documents, the name was used immediately in the August 1878 War Congress where it is recorded that the Mission had "organized a salvation army to carry the blood of Christ and the fire of the Holy Ghost into every corner of the world."[4] The pamphlet that bore the name change explained, "The Christian Mission, under the superintendence of Rev. William Booth, is a Salvation Army recruited from among the multitudes who are without God and without hope in the world, devoting their leisure time to all sorts of laborious efforts for the salvation of others from unbelief, drunkenness, vice and crime."[5] Remarking on the combination of faith and apparent foolishness of these declarations, Salvation Army historian Robert Sandall reports, "the new Army had in the whole of England but fifty stations, manned by eighty–eight evangelists; and elsewhere—nothing!"[6]

It seems to have been an idea that not only captured the imagination but mobilized people, particularly given the climate created by expanding Christianity. While the name Christian Mission was a good one, the name Salvation Army was a galvanizing one. The ability to develop military themes around this name was endless. It provided the framework for an aggressive Christianity. If Queen Victoria could with confidence look on her powerful military, how much more could the Lord delight in His newly commissioned army?

Writing about the new name, William Booth declared, "What a strange name! What does it mean? Just what it says—a number of people joined together after the fashion of an army; and therefore it is an army, and an army for the purpose of carrying Salvation through the land, neither more nor less than that."[7]

More than rhetoric, the name changed the character of the organization from description to dynamism. Later Bramwell Booth recalled that the Founder could find no scriptural reason not to pursue the military form.[8]

Something New

Forming The Salvation Army represented more than a reorganization. It created something the world had never seen. First, it took the ancient structure of the military, a form that has been virtually unchanged throughout history. Although the names of ranks have changed in conformity with the language, the structure has remained consistent, with commanders over small groups, which in turn are part of larger groups with a commander, which in turn are part of still larger groups with a commander at the head. Existing in every culture, country and civilization with but cosmetic changes, the military forms a near perfect organizational structure. Though the kingdoms they defended have risen and fallen, the military form remains.

The second ancient structure was the Christian Church. Formed to carry the message of redemption throughout the world, the Church has endured fierce persecution from outside and corruption from within. Though not without its faults, it remains the primary vehicle of grace in a fallen world. William Booth was not opposed to the tradition of the Church's redemptive mission but impatient with the forms that sometimes obscured its primary purpose.

In The Salvation Army these two forms were united for the first time. The purpose was not to form an arm of the Church, as had been the case with the Jesuits, but to raise up an army that stood alone, free to attack sin where it was found and to enlist all whose cleansed hearts equipped them for service. It could be described as Christianity in battle fatigues.

It didn't take the Army long to exploit the power of this new form. William Booth realized that this was something that required explaining. "Does all this sound strange, dear brother—not sacred, not ecclesiastical, not according to the traditions of the elders, and after the pattern of existing things and institutions? Is it something new? It may be so, and yet it may be none the less true and scriptural, and none the less of divine origin and made after some heavenly pattern for all that."[9]

Distinctly Salvation Army

One of the first distinctions was the uniform. Again Elijah Cadman had anticipated this development. He wrote, "I would like to wear a suit of clothes that would let everyone know I meant war to the teeth and salvation for the world."[10] On the other side of the debate was George Scott Railton, who feared uniforms might create a separation that would keep Salvationists apart from other people, much like the parish priest's robes separated him from his congregation.[11]

Despite Railton's misgivings, the majority sided with Cadman. At first, The Salvation Army's least uniform aspect was the uniform itself. A dizzying array was created out of former military uniforms, firemen's helmets and adapted coats and tails. Caps might be pillbox, pith helmets, derbies or any headgear that could hold a Salvation Army pin or placard. The first officially approved uniform with ladies' headgear was unveiled at the farewell meeting for the pioneer officers heading off to the United States in 1880. Booth's satisfaction with the effect of the uniform was confirmed by his statement that the uniform was "very useful, attracts attention, gives opportunity for conversation, gathers people together at the open–air demonstrations, excites respect in the rowdy population, indicates not only connection with the Army but the person's position in it, and is a safeguard against conformity to the fashions of the day."[12] Further, the uniform eliminated class distinctions. It provided the sense of empowerment, especially appreciated by those who had known so little of that in their lives.

The uniform has become an enduring symbol of The Salvation Army, not only for the public but for the Salvationist as well. To many Salvationists the uniform is a treasured possession identifying what they have become. Uganda's dictator, Idi Amin, persecuted Christians in his country, including forcing the Army to disband. Commissioner Stanley Walter wrote, "It was during my stay in East Africa (1978–82) that General Idi Amin ordered the cessation of Salvation Army work in Uganda. Following Amin's overthrow, soldiers joyfully retrieved their uniforms and song books from their hiding places (often underground) and the work was resumed."[13]

The first flags were designed and sewn by Catherine Booth, the Army Mother. The symbol in the center was a sun, but it was later changed to the present–day star, since in India the sun was a sacred symbol. Flags were presented to the American pioneering party to complete the military bearing of an invasion force. Catherine Baird, Salvation Army poet extraordinaire as well as gifted author, wrote about the importance of The Salvation Army flag:

> Flags, or ancient standards, have been found among the remains of the earliest civilizations. Archaeologists have unearthed sculptures that prove the Egyptians, Assyrians, Persians, as well as the Hebrews, had standards. In Numbers 2:2 we read: "Every man of the children of Israel shall pitch by his own standard, with the ensign of their father's house." But little is known about these standards and ensigns.

> Early flags, however, were almost always of religious character, and designs show that religious emblems were employed to give dignity and authority to national flags. Thus, a banner bearing a sacred sign like the Cross of Jesus could be borne into an unholy battle.

> But the Salvation Army banner has no other name and sign than the symbols of God's redeeming love which cannot be superimposed on another emblem or combined with it. Therefore the Salvationist who carries the Army flag engages in a holy war against sin. He cannot and would not try to equate the world with God. As long as he marches behind the yellow, red and blue, his aim must be to live for God who was "in Christ reconciling the world unto Himself."[14]

Military terminology came into common use as Mission evangelists were transformed into officers of various ranks. Members were soldiers, stations became corps. Perhaps one of the most interesting changes surrounded the hymnody of the Army. Though the Army was ready to use traditional hymns if they were lively enough, members formed their own songs, readily borrowing tunes from the pubs or adapting folk tunes with words appropriate for less polished audiences. But it was because the Army had a sense of its own unique identity and mission in the world that it began to sing about itself, a musical phenomenon not seen before. The first song to actually incorporate the name of The Salvation Army was set to the tune "Ring the Bell, Watchman."

> *Come, join our Army, to battle we go,*
> *Jesus will help us to conquer the foe;*
> *Fighting for right and opposing the wrong,*
> *The Salvation Army is marching along.*[15]

Another song that represents The Salvation Army's sense of itself and its mission says:

> *Jesus, give Thy blood–washed Army*
> *Universal liberty;*
> *Keep us fighting, trusting calmly*
> *For a worldwide jubilee.*
> *Hallelujah!*
> *We shall have the victory.*
>
> *Lift up valleys, cast down mountains,*
> *Make all evil natures good;*
> *Wash the world in Calvary's fountain,*
> *Send us a great salvation flood.*
> *All the nations!*
> *We shall win with fire and blood.*[16]

In an interesting development, Salvationists began publishing editions of the Bible with the *Song Book* inserted. Though some might treat the Bible with more deference, the Army considered it practical to combine the two. It did not lessen the truth of the Scriptures, and for many the *Song Book* was beloved next to the Bible.

The military theme led naturally to the new Army embracing brass bands, a treasured feature of British military for years. The first such band was formed not by The Salvation Army, but by members of the

Fryfamily in Salisbury, England, who were sympathetic to the Salvationists. Witnessing that they were often attacked during their open–air meetings, the Frys decided to protect them from these coward-ly attacks. When four of the family members were discovered to be expert musicians, the corps officer persuaded them to bring their instruments to the open–air meeting. Soon after that, they became Salvationists, and so The Salvation Army had its first band. When the Founder heard the report, he traveled to Salisbury and pronounced his blessing. The deci-sion was made to promote the formation of brass bands.[17] The bands caught on rapidly although their early complexion tended to stretch the concept of a well–defined musical group. Nonetheless, the bands added to the military mood of the Army and became a permanent part of its ministry and identity.

To many outside the movement it was fearful to watch the develop-ment of The Salvation Army and the fierce loyalty that it often engen-dered from its followers. Yet in the study of James C. Collins and Jerry I. Parros of visionary companies that had a track record of success over long periods of time, the parallel to what developed in The Salvation Army is remarkable. They write:

> The visionary companies don't merely declare an ideology; they also take steps to make the ideology pervasive through-out the organization and transcend the individual leader.
>
> - The visionary companies more thoroughly indoctrinate employees into a core ideology . . . creating cultures so strong that they are almost cult–like around the ideology.
>
> - The visionary companies more carefully nurture and select senior management based on their fit with a core ideology.
>
> - The visionary companies attain more consistent align-ment with a core ideology—in such aspects as goals, strategy, tactics, and organization design.[18]

The Enemy Attacks

With even the songs reflecting the unique nature of the Army, it was no small surprise that Booth would encourage Railton to look, not to ecclesiastical sources, but to military ones for guidelines as to how to operate this new creation. "It is a remarkable fact that our system corresponds so closely to that of the army and navy of this country that we have been able to use even the very words of many of their regulations."[19] Not surprisingly, the switch to a military system caused considerable reaction outside the Army. For many it made the Army an easy target for derision and disdain. When writing his name, most reporters refused to acknowledge the title of General for William Booth, choosing instead to place quotation marks around the title. (It wasn't until the Queen of England addressed him without the quotes around *General* that this practice stopped.) More than that, the Army and Booth were parodied in cartoons and in the editorial columns. On the streets derisive songs were sung about the Army, many of them derived from the songs Salvationists used.

Of greater concern was a climate of widespread and sometimes violent persecution that for a time became the lot of Salvationists. Army corps were attacked by gangs and people assaulted in the meetings. But it was far worse in the open–air meetings. There the soldiers were in full sight of the roughest elements. Rather than finding protection from the police, Salvationists were often cited for disturbing the peace. Thousands were jailed, not only in Britain but also in other countries where the Army soon spread.

"The Skeleton Army," a group using pirates' skull and crossbones flags, ranks, and uniforms that mimicked the Army, tried to intimidate Salvationists to the extent that they would abandon their profession. These groups were often financed by pub owners and others who found the Army disruptive to their trade. Sadly, some support came from the religious community who found the Army's ways vulgar and heretical. Typical of the critics of the day, one wrote, "Its [the Army's] autocratic and military system has become a fetish. The adoption of military titles, organization and methods in religious warfare is imposing, but their utility is a mere delusion."[20]

A contemporary report from that period gives some indication of the violence. What follows occurred one day in one place. But the experience was commonplace throughout Britain, Europe, and the United States:

> The agitation still continued; the mob gathered every evening. I remember one Sunday afternoon whilst passing along North Street [Guildford, England] we were furiously attacked; blows were struck and sticks freely used. Happy

Mary, who was present, received much rough usage, and we had great difficulty in getting safely to our barracks. She [Happy Mary] received such a shock at the time that she sank in health, left the station soon after, and in a week she was dead.[21]

Respect and Replication

Not everyone found the Army something to dismiss. W. T. Stead, early friend of Booth and editor of the respected *Pall Mall Gazette,* wrote:

The Salvation Army is a phenomenon, look at it how we may, that is of enormous, almost unequaled importance . . . an object lesson on which we shall do well to ponder; a revelation, the full significance of which has been but imperfectly appreciated; and a great concrete fact which may contain hidden within it the key to the solution of many of the most perplexing problems which confront the modern world. . . . To us the supreme distinction of The Salvation Army is that it has done more to realize the ideals of almost every social reformer, secular or religious, than any other organization we can name. . . . The fraternity of men, the enfranchisement of women, the greater simplicity of life, the obligation of altruistic service, the combination of democratic equality with the enforcement of autocratic discipline, the duty of temperance, the recognition of the need for social intercourse—all these find in The Salvation Army more practical realization and more effective recognition than elsewhere. . . . General Booth has done more to secure the attainment by this generation of the goal of human effort than all authorities put together.[22]

The success of The Salvation Army was also noticed by the Anglican Church. At one time negotiations between Booth and leaders of that church discussed the possibility of incorporating The Salvation Army as a branch of the church. The offer was tempting, for although the Army was spreading rapidly throughout the world, finances were precarious on the best days. To have the resources of the Anglican Church and its backing would not only provide the means but the respect that were both in short supply.

The negotiations broke down. For his part, Booth was unwilling to see the Army hampered in its freedom to move as it would. For their part, the Anglicans could not accept the ordination of women nor the Army's unorthodox view of the sacraments (see Chapter 5).[23] Although the partnership did not work out, the Church still flattered Booth in the sincerest way.

In 1882, the Anglican Church established the Church Army under the direction of Wilson Carlile. It copied the Army's uniforms, songs, terminology, and open–air meetings.[24] It also suffered alongside The Salvation Army as it was targeted by the criminal element, including the Skeleton Army.[25] Although it spread to other countries, its largest following and influence remained in Britain, where it continues to operate today.

Imitation by the Anglicans was one of the more honorable that occurred. An unforeseen result of the novel Salvation Army was the large number of counterfeits and copies that sprang up. Most of these were local expressions like the one in Sacramento, California, reporting that "[W. E. Purdy] has adopted a uniform which is the counterpart worn by Salvationists, save a few minor details." The problem for the Army was the confusion created in the public mind between the counterfeits and the real Army. Unfortunately, many of these counterfeits recognized the Army's fundraising ability and mimicked it for this reason. Others, while operating with sincere motive, were injurious because they often failed to hold the same high standards that the Army imposed upon itself. The imitation of The Salvation Army over the years is one of the most unique problems faced by the organization. One is never confronted with an imitation Presbyterian or Methodist church, but the Army's distinctive nature makes it vulnerable to imitation.

Clarity and Confusion

Nevertheless, the strengths of the Army's system have been lasting. As mentioned earlier, the military system translates to all cultures and provides a framework that explains how the Army functions. The military structure has allowed the Army to maintain its flexibility and to respond quickly when called upon. Its symbolism remains fascinating to those both inside and outside the movement. Lord Hattersley, British author and member of Parliament, writes:

> [The Salvation Army] still looks part of the past not the
> future. Part of the problem is the uniform and the slightly
> absurd military ranks. But they are also the Army's greatest

strength—the visible proclamation of fixed principles in a time of shifting values. They are essential to a process called bearing witness and, as any public relations consultant would confirm, that is about as unfashionable an occupation as it is possible to promote. . . . Whenever I see The Salvation Army on parade I ask myself who is benefiting from the banging drums. The answer is the men and women who bang them. They know whose side they are on. In the case of The Salvation Army it is the side of God and the poor.[26]

A military structure is more conducive to changes in strategy. It is understood that, while an army may go to battle with a specific plan, battles are not fought under ideal conditions. The enemy moves in a way not expected or an opening occurs where not expected. In addition, commanders who may be wonderful at preparing troops may not be the best to lead them. Sometimes unexpected leaders emerge and these are the ones who must lead the troops forward. What is evident in an earthly battle certainly is true in the spiritual realm as well. For an army to function, it must be able change tactics. By casting the organization in a military mold, this is more readily understood. It answers the question: "Once you know the right thing, do you have the discipline to do the right thing, and, equally important, quit doing the wrong thing?"[27]

Problems also can arise in a military structure. Because there is no other organization like it, The Salvation Army is often misunderstood. Explaining the Army to the uninitiated can take time and great effort. Also, because it doesn't necessarily look like a traditional religious organization, it can be mistaken for not being one.

In some cultures where the military is held in low regard, the appeal of The Salvation Army's military pattern can be limited, hindering recruitment. In totalitarian lands or in countries where roving armies of rebels fight against the government the Army can be viewed as a competitor. The Salvation Army with its military uniforms has often found itself banished from countries for this very reason.

Despite ridicule and misunderstanding, the Army's system continues to function efficiently. Its peculiarities annoy some, inspire others and fascinate nearly all when they first encounter it. It remains a constant metaphor of Christianity in action.

Internationalism

If The Salvation Army flag were compiled from all the national flags in which it serves, its symbols would range from spears to guns, stars to suns, crosses to crescents, lions to rattlesnakes. The colors would be a splendid rainbow with the Army colors of yellow, red, and blue linking them all together. Such a flag would represent one of the greatest miracles of The Salvation Army—its internationalism.

When William and Catherine Booth began work in London their original intent was to make an impact for God on the East End of London. But the compelling nature of the Christian Mission carried it across England's countryside. The spread beyond London was a pleasing development, but it complicated administration for Booth. He and the early leaders were torn by the problems and promises that came with expansion.

Financing the work was a constant concern. When it was difficult to pay the bills for the operations as they stood, expansion only created more. They handled the problem by moving ahead anyway. Pioneer officers were sent to towns, usually with only enough money to obtain lodgings and meals for a few days. After that they were on their own to raise enough money to establish the work by obtaining a suitable building, and paying for *The War Cry* order and other essentials to organizing a fighting force. They were required to forward to headquarters a tithe of all the money raised. Officers could draw their meager allowance from any money remaining after all bills were paid. It was financing by grit and grace.

Complicating Army expansion was personnel. Many of that first generation of officers were teenagers, most of them female. What they lacked in experience they compensated for with energy and enthusiasm. But there remains no substitute for experience. Losses were high. Some left to marry while others suffered breakdowns in health due to the heavy demands of the work. Some struggled with the Army structure or were bothered by an assortment of objections to Army life including women in authority, doctrinal issues, the Sacraments, and the difference between their ambitious goals for themselves and their actual positions. But many of these youthful warriors showed tremendous heroism and ingenuity. As in any war, it was the youth who fought hardest on the front lines.

Booth often lamented that operations could begin in hundreds of other places if only he had the people to send. The desperation for workers is clear in the plea by the Field Secretary: "Men! Men! Men! Oh, my God, send us men! Never mind if you do stammer, or if you have a wooden leg, or a weak chest, or if you have only one eye, or have no platform ability. If you are a Salvation Army soldier, and have brains, energy, tact and business ability, don't let this appeal haunt you till you write the Field Secretary straight away."[1] The immediacy of the need is found in William Booth's challenge, "Make your will, pack your box, kiss your girl, be ready in a week."[2]

Added to this was the tremendous persecution Salvationists were enduring. In some places it seemed that the Army had no sooner held its first meeting than the enemies began their assault. As often as not, opposition began forming at the mere mention that The Salvation Army was coming to town. When the Salvationists prepared to "open fire" (the military metaphor for starting an Army work), opposition dogged their every step as some determined to end this nuisance before it gained a foothold. When Booth declared war on sin, Satan retaliated by drawing blood from the Salvation shock troops.

Unintended Invasion

Amid all of this, Eliza Shirley, a sixteen year old who showed great promise, announced her plans in 1879 to immigrate to America with her family. William Booth himself met with her to ask her to stay in London. To his surprise she not only held firm with her plans to go but surprised him by asking for permission to start The Salvation Army work across the Atlantic. This was not what Booth wanted to hear. His hands were full with Britain and he did not have the highest opinion of the United States with its brash and independent people. But Shirley pressed him and he reluctantly agreed that she could start the work using the Army name. If she met with success he would consider making the work official and perhaps send reinforcements.

This was not the first time an international expansion had been considered. In 1870 a Christian Mission convert named James Jermy opened a branch of the Christian Mission in Cleveland, Ohio. After the filing of some reports with *The Christian Mission Evangelist,* there was no further mention, and the work ceased.

But Eliza Shirley's venture was successful and Booth had to face what it meant to command a force that could not be held to the British Isles. He sent George Scott Railton and seven single women whom Railton dubbed the "Splendid Seven." Following a rousing meeting, the party was launched. In 1880 The Salvation Army became an international concern, and the opening in the States fired the imagination to carry the Salvation War to other countries.

Initially the international expansion was guided by two primary criteria: geographic proximity to either Great Britain or to the colonies in the British Empire (with the United States being a notable exception). Near neighbors first invaded by the Army included France, Switzerland and Sweden. The British Empire furnished access to India, Canada, South Africa, and Australia. Norman Murdoch, professor of history at the University of Cincinnati, notes, "By 1888, overseas expansion made The Salvation Army the world's fastest growing Christian sect in an age of missions." [3]

Although the idea had been developing since the first days in the East End of London, it was during this period of initial international expansion that The Salvation Army's core idea of winning the world for Christ was clarified. It can be said that this driving notion so possessed Salvationists that the Army no longer needed the direct supervision of the Founder. The very idea was enough to give clear direction and purpose as the Army leaped over national boundaries and crossed oceans. Although the ideal was later damaged by two devastating world wars, it remained the guiding star that defined not only the Army's destiny but in large part its development. Much later, the unspoken rediscovery of that ideal once again renewed and re-energized the Army.

The original idea of saving the world for Christ was heavily influenced by a view held by many evangelical Christians at the time that the spread of the gospel would continue until all the people of the world were reached, after which Christ would return to rule the world. Because of the rapid advance of evangelical Christianity and the quickening pace of the missionary movement, the winning of the world to Christ seemed imminently attainable. But allegiance to this theology cannot fully explain the dynamism of Salvationists. They believed firmly that if one person could be saved at any time anywhere from any sin, all people in all places could be saved. The world could be laid at Jesus' feet.

Take Off Your Boots

It wasn't until the Army reached into India, however, that it first encountered a largely non–Christian culture. Frederick Tucker had been a highly positioned and well–paid civil servant of the British government in India. One day he happened upon a copy of *The War Cry*, the Army's official publication, and was fascinated with what he read. He became convinced that The Salvation Army could be the means to reach the largely Hindu and Muslim populations of India. Traveling to London, he offered himself for service as a Salvation Army officer and presented a plan for how the Army could work in his adopted land. Though distrustful of the well–educated and the wealthy who offered themselves for service, William Booth listened to Tucker's proposal.

Tucker related what he had heard from a native Indian. "We will not believe until the English man removes his boots and walks barefoot." The problem with Christian outreach as Tucker saw it, was that missionaries not only wanted to convert the Indian people to Christianity but wanted to Westernize them as well. The Indian people were proud of their ancient culture and were extremely resistant to any idea that their civilization was in any way inferior to the one introduced by the British. To answer this, Tucker suggested that the Army not enter India wearing the dark serge uniforms of Western society, but the saris of India. Further, they should abandon their Christian names for Indian names, their Western ways for those of the people. With his heart for the poor, Tucker further proposed that the style of dress should be that worn by the lowest caste in India. Here he felt the Army might find the greatest opening since they were the ones most deprived in the Hindu system. Booth approved the plan and the invasion of India proceeded.

The ideas introduced by Tucker would be copied by other pioneering officers among the Zulus in South Africa, the Buddhists of Sri Lanka

(Ceylon), the Japanese, and others. This sensitivity to the culture was a different approach than that employed by other religious organizations of the day. The Salvationists enjoyed some success, but it was far more modest than in countries having a Christian culture. Nor was the success universal. Predominantly Catholic countries were resistant to all Protestant incursions, including The Salvation Army.

An example of what the early pioneers faced is found in the memories of Lt. Colonel Jacob G. Brouwer concerning the opening of the Army work in the Dutch East Indies, now Indonesia:

> We were assured that God would guide and provide and that His grace would be sufficient. Thus, on November 24, 1894, two pioneer officers landed at Batavia (now Jakarta). Little notice was taken of them. Only a few cast curious and rather pitying looks at them. They doubtless felt what one of the chief officials soon afterward expressed, that in this prosperous colony, "with its idyllic conditions, there was no need for The Salvation Army." No need for The Salvation Army? What of the lepers, the blind, the other victims of eye diseases, the uncared–for children, the fallen women and all the sick and destitute? . . . Of course, very few in those early days knew the spiritual strength of the Army; nor did they realize what the Spirit of Christ, working in and through simple, consecrated men and women, could accomplish.[4]

Nor have the efforts to spread the Army internationally been limited to those from Western countries. In northern Myanmar, Salvationists of Mizo origin independently established The Salvation Army in this remotest of regions. Myanmar Salvationists established themselves, raising corps buildings and hand crafting uniforms and flags before notifying the Army of their work and desire to be recognized by The Salvation Army.[5] This stellar effort has led to northern Myanmar becoming one of the international Army's fastest growing fields of work in the beginning of the twenty–first century.

Cultural Realities

The Army also found that many countries' laws protected the predominant or state religions and severely limited the functioning of Christian bodies. The introduction of social work not only gave the

Army a means to serve the people in a practical way but also provided an entry into otherwise hostile environments. Governments were willing to tolerate in some measure the Christian message of the Army because they needed the hospitals, clinics, schools, children's homes and shelters that were established.

The realities of work across nations and cultures continues to be a challenge for The Salvation Army. Initially accustomed to the non–interference of the state in religious exercise, the Salvationists found, as Harvard University professor Samuel P. Huntington has written, "only in Hindu civilization were religion and politics also distinctly separated. In Islam, God is Caesar; in China and Japan, Caesar is God; in Orthodoxy, God is Caesar's junior partner."[6] This has made The Salvation Army in many places very much an outsider.

The Army would also soon find out how precarious its position was when the fortunes of nations changed. Soon after the Bolshevik Revolution in 1917 the Army was outlawed in Russia. This would be repeated in country after country with communist governments. Work would eventually be extinguished in Latvia, Estonia, Hungary, Czechoslovakia, East Germany, and China, to name a few. In other places, the instability of governments would cause working conditions for the Army to go from good to bad. In Latin America the Army was forced at times to discontinue its work or to suffer banishment.

In some places the continuance of the work is always a question. Although the Army is not operating in the whole Muslim world, it is established in several countries with a predominantly Muslim population. Indonesia, Pakistan, Bangladesh, and others appreciate the Army's social ministry and have allowed it some freedom to operate. However, as Muslim fundamentalism continues to spread and with it strong anti–Western sentiment, The Salvation Army may be restricted either by government or by the actions of individuals or terrorist organizations that view Christian ministries as a threat. Indonesia and Pakistan in particular are vying for a leading position in the Muslim world. It is not unusual for leaders to take actions against Christian organizations, not because they personally feel it is needed but because it "plays to the gallery" to segments of their populations.

In a similar vein, in Russia and the other nations of the Commonwealth of Independent States the standing of the Army is threatened by the Orthodox Church, the traditional faith in this area of the world. Actions in Russia along this line in 2001 almost closed The Salvation Army after its reopening there only a few years earlier. Moscow courts decided in the Army's favor, but the action confirms that the Army can and will find itself targeted from time to time.

Rampant nationalism poses an additional danger. It showed itself in the United States when first Thomas Moore and then Ballington Booth fostered schisms from the international movement (see Chapter 2). The overt patriotism of the ascendant American republic bumped into the British assertion that it was not yet ready to relinquish its position of leadership in the world. The resulting friction caused the Americans to look for a battleground in sometimes unlikely places. Although several issues affected the Army in both of these breaks, nationalism merged with the strongly anti–British sentiment of the day to fuel emotions. Later in Mexico, an abortive attempt was made to form a Mexican Salvation Army apart from the parent organization. This latter attempt would have been successful had not loyal Mexican Salvationists prevented it. Existing Mexican law would have favored the dissenters, leaving the Army no recourse but to start over. Coupled with the loyalty of Salvationists, steps have been taken to ensure that such an action does not take place in Mexico again.

But Mexico is not alone in fostering laws that actually encourage and protect those who would "nationalize" The Salvation Army. With the end of the Cold War the West has lost some of its influence. This may embolden those who view the international Salvation Army as a Western operation against their own nationalistic interests, leaving the international brotherhood of the Army as a casualty. General Albert Orsborn remarked on the Army's challenge with these realities:

> Unto this present day, our remarkable federation of Salvation Army units, partially but in no case wholly autonomous, crossing all boundaries, speaking all languages, devoted to the Kingdom of God and bound in one faith under one flag and one General, has held together without loss excepting in lands where hostile governments have suppressed us. This is very remarkable in a world where nationalism has the fervor of a religion, and fragmentations and barriers are defenses.[7]

Men and Money

Some of the problems Booth faced, such as shortage of funds and personnel, still remain. In most of the countries where the Army operates, it is subsidized in both money and leadership. Soldier and officer training that might help territories and commands to move toward greater self–sufficiency are limited by available resources. Officers and employees sometimes find it difficult to live on what is provided for them. In some prosperous nations, the sacrifice of officership compared to the promise of a career in the secular world frustrates efforts to become self–sufficient. In some cultures it is an unknown concept to provide public support for organizations like The Salvation Army.

The lack of funds for much of the world can also cause some misunderstanding between those in developed countries and those in developing countries. It can be assumed by those in developed countries that they operate at a higher level of efficiency. Further, it can be thought that resources readily available to them are as accessible elsewhere. On the other hand, those in developing countries may feel that the wealth of other nations prevents them from knowing what it is to sacrifice. It is good for all to remember that regardless of where Salvationists are, there is work and challenge relative to the place of service.

In recent years, World Services funds administered by International Headquarters have been strained beyond limits. The needs are far too great while the income is far too small. The result is that many valid needs remain unmet, and International Headquarters has been forced to wean supported territories and commands from World Services financial support. Some countries have become too reliant on the international Army to sustain their work while not fully exploiting their ability to raise funds locally. When a territory looks within its own country for support, a further maturation of the local Army can take place. But it is often a painful process.

For All People

Given these potential problems, how has the Army prospered as an international movement? It has been proven over the years that Salvationism transcends culture. Although the mechanisms of the Army vary greatly, the spirit that drives it remains the same. Wisely, it was decided to encourage interaction between the different peoples of the Army. This has ranged from huge international Congresses to visits by individuals. Another venue is the International College for Officers that brings officers together from across the world for eight–week sessions and furnishes valuable education and opportunities to meet their peers from other cultures and ethnic groups. Personnel exchanges, both officer and lay, also strengthen international ties, allowing individuals to experience the realities and challenges of a different culture. These opportunities give Salvationists the chance to form relationships and bond with others who serve under the same flag.

That spirit of internationalism was no more beautifully displayed than at the International Leaders' Conference in 1984, held in the then divided city of Berlin. As Salvation Army leaders from around the world crossed into East Berlin, they stopped at the Reformed Church where they were met by the Lutheran Bishop of East Berlin for his prayer of blessing on the Army. Henry Gariepy described what followed :

> Then it happened—an electric moment indelibly inscribed on the heart of each one present. Spontaneously, the Salvationists broke into singing in their own languages Booth's "O Boundless Salvation." The strains echoed their deep feelings throughout the sanctuary of the great church, irrepressibly pouring forth . . . their hearts. All their diversities and differences in that moment were transcended by their union in Christ, eloquently expressed in the words penned by the Founder and inspired by his world vision for God and the Army.

> If the singing did not have the fine musicianship which usually marks Army renderings, it was because voices . . . choked with emotion and fervency care little for musicianship at such times.[8]

The organic unity of The Salvation Army also contributes to the Army's internationalism. With the possible exception of the Catholic Church, no religious organization is as unified on an international level. There is one General whose influence is recognized the world over. With the leader rests the authority to appoint individuals and to support, monitor and advance the work. Given the vast changes in the world's landscape since its East London beginnings, the Army's continued unity is a great wonder.

The Army has worked hard to maintain this unity. Publications such as *Orders and Regulations, Salvation Story* and approved local editions of The Salvation Army *Song Book* ensure uniformity in teaching and practice.[9] International publications such as *All the World* and *The Officer* bring Salvationists together. Similarly, reviews and inspections by International Headquarters provide consistency. Given the natural bent for societies to drift in their own directions, these efforts are key to preserving the tradition of internationalism.

Although organic unity is important, the Army has also attempted to allow cultural expression within the broad guidelines it has outlined. This explains in part the explosive growth in some parts of the world. When Africa was dominated by European powers, the Army's growth was steady but slow. When the Africans obtained self–government and colonial influence weakened, the Army began to enjoy phenomenal growth. Nowhere can this be seen more clearly than in what is now Zimbabwe and the East Africa Territory. With worship styles reflective of their culture and far different from those found in Great Britain or Canada, the Africans are leading the way in evangelism and growth. They are very much African while remaining very much Salvation Army.

The most basic problem that threatens internationalism is when one culture tries to impose itself upon another. This can be the danger with reinforcement and secondment personnel. No matter how much an American might insist, the Japanese are not going to abandon their culture. There is no "one size fits all" in the world today. In a word, colonialism is dead. If anything, ancient cultures are reemerging as was seen in the disintegration of the nation of Yugoslavia and the Soviet Union. While the truth must never be sacrificed, the manner in which it is applied cannot be dictated in absolute fashion. While the water remains pure, the shape of the vessel can vary greatly.

Similarly, when people in receiving cultures fail to value the contributions of others, they deny themselves the experience of those who have come and miss a learning experience for themselves. It is not surprising that a receiving culture would be naturally resistant to "outsiders," but in a world that is experiencing international relations on both the macro and micro levels, to remain isolated is to risk falling behind.

The internationalism of the Army provides it with tremendous richness. Though very different, the Army around the world is very much the same through Christ. This unity under one flag is one of the Army's greatest miracles.

The Sacraments

The Salvation Army's position on the sacraments took it down a largely unexplored road. The definition of the power of salvation and the nature of the Christian life became a turning point for the Army.

William Booth proved that he was as undaunted by controversy as he was unconvinced by arguments from tradition. It was not enough that women preach; they must be placed in positions of authority. Not satisfied to simply lead; he abolished the democratic process. Unrestrained by ecclesiastical structure, he marshaled his troops into an army. Nineteen centuries of Church tradition were not enough to deter him from questioning one of its most honored rituals.

While the initial organization of the Army was radically different from Booth's Methodist beginnings, the doctrines and practices he brought into the Movement were not. He clung to the teachings of his hero of the faith, John Wesley. From this heritage he both claimed and taught the blessing of holiness. His heart echoed with Wesley that he was a man of one Book. And in establishing the worship of the Christian Mission he accepted the place given to the Protestant sacraments of the Lord's Supper (communion) and infant baptism by sprinkling.

Booth administered infant baptism according to the tradition of the Methodist church. It was the tradition sanctioned by the Anglicans and Catholics as well as by some non–conformist churches. Though widely accepted, infant baptism never figured importantly in the life of the Army. Emphasis was placed on an individual's willful conversion, not on a formal ceremony inducting them into the Church.[1] Adult baptism was considered unnecessary because of the drama of the salvation experience.[2]

The Lord's Supper was also practiced. It was freely administered monthly in Christian Missions stations to all members and Christian friends in good standing.[3]

Dr. Roger Green, Salvationist author and chair of Biblical Studies at Gordon College in Massachusetts, relates Miss Jane Short's deeply moving experience concerning the Lord's Supper and the mother of Catherine Booth as she lay dying:

> In those days the Booths had not given up the communion service, and towards the last, poor Mrs. Mumford, who had suffered untold agonies from cancer, asked that the General should give her the sacrament. I was present then . . . and I cannot tell you how deeply I was affected by the beautiful tenderness of the General on that occasion. He made one feel that the whole service was deeply personal to the poor dying woman; he put his arm about her, bent his face close to hers, and said—I shall never forget—"Take and eat this, Mother, in remembrance of that Christ's blood was shed for thee," and his voice, though it trembled with tenderness, was strong in faith. . . . Her death was remarkable. Mrs. Booth was kneeling at her side, holding her hand, and quite suddenly Mrs. Mumford regained consciousness, opened her eyes wide, and with a light on her face that was unearthly, exclaimed, "Kate!—Jesus!" and was gone in that moment.[4]

A Simpler Salvation

If it could have remained that simple, the Army's practice concerning the sacraments might not have changed. Division over the matter entered the Church at large, including the Army. Since the days of the Protestant Reformation there had been spirited debate regarding the exact theological meaning and proper administration of the sacraments. Catholic and High Church parties held to a view that baptism was in itself an act of grace, in which salvation was conferred on the person. They further held, with some degree of interpretation, that in the elements of the Lord's Supper, Christ's body and blood were present. Other traditions held that the sacraments were symbolic of inward acts of grace. Baptism was thus considered to be a testimony. For an infant it indicated the parents' desire for their child to grow up as a Christian. For adults, it signified their new life in Christ. The Lord's Supper was indicative of the spiritual vitality of the believer and identification with the suffering and death of Christ.

Even though there was agreement that these sacraments should be practiced, there was disagreement as to the virtue of infant versus adult baptism, or if the sacrament could involve sprinkling or required immersion. As to the Lord's Supper, disagreements arose over whether grape juice was a permissible substitute for wine, if the act was symbolic or if Christ was actually present in the elements. The differences of opinion started over these broad matters and splintered into many smaller ones. Booth had little tolerance for quarrels of this sort.[5]

Apparently what finally forced the issue were the discussions of merger with the Church of England (see Chapter 4). Roger Green relates the wide–ranging, often heated discussions that involved William and Catherine Booth, Bramwell Booth and George Scott Railton. "How many sacraments? Who could administer them? Was Christ fully present at the Lord's Supper or only symbolically present? How often should the Lord's Supper be taken by the faithful? Should sinners be invited to the communion rail as John Wesley had done in the previous century?"[6]

The example of the Society of Friends (Quakers) had proven that vital Christian fellowship could be had without the sacraments.[7] Perhaps influenced by divisions in the church or their own mystical leanings, Catherine Booth and George Scott Railton questioned the necessity of the sacraments in the life of the Army as a whole and the believer in particular. Catherine Booth had "a deep horror of anything which might tend to substitute in the minds of the people some outward act or compliance for the fruits of practical holiness."[8] In one sermon she outlined this belief:

> [A] mock salvation is presented in the shape of ceremonies and sacraments. . . . Men are taught that by going through them or partaking of them, they are to be saved. . . . What an inveterate tendency there is in the human heart to trust in outward forms, instead of seeking the inward grace! And where this is the case, what a hindrance rather than help have these forms proved to the growth, nay, to the very existence of that spiritual life which constitutes the real and only force of Christian experience.[9]

Of greater import to the Army was the question of women administering the sacraments. Colonel Brian Tuck, noted South African Salvation Army officer and teacher, notes that the Army was the first in the history of the Church to allow women to administer the sacraments.[10] That advance notwithstanding, Bramwell Booth recalled, "the idea of women administrating the sacraments was at that time almost unthinkable to many good people."[11] To mollify decided public opinion and the feelings of the majority of their people, would they deny women the right to administer the sacraments? How could the standard of equality be upheld under these circumstances?

The use of wine in the Lord's Supper posed another obstacle. Non–alcoholic grape juice, so commonly used today by many churches, was unavailable in Britain at this time.[12] To use wine was unthinkable, given the large numbers of Salvationists who had been saved from alcoholism. For them the sight, taste or even the smell might be enough to send them back into a life of drinking.[13] To trade off a man or woman's soul for a ceremony was too high a price.

Another ground for questioning the use of the sacraments centered around the nature of The Salvation Army. Appealing to its unique nature, Booth distanced the Army further from existing denominations. He later recalled, "We came into this position originally by determining not to be a church. We did not wish to undertake the administration of the sacraments, and thereby bring ourselves into collision with existing churches."[14] Further, the Church of England took the position that Salvation Army soldiers could not participate in communion because they had not been confirmed in the church.[15]

The statement that the Army did not constitute a church was reasonable from one standpoint. The Army's mission was to the unchurched, many of whom had felt alienated from the Church and avoided anything that resembled religious formalism. What seems not to have been taken into consideration, or at least admitted, is that for the thousands then attending, the Army was their church. It was where they were saved and testified to it, where they sang and prayed and preached and taught. They were married in Salvation Army meetings and buried using Salvation Army ceremonies. Although it might not have looked at all like the traditional church in its forms, it served as a church in its function. If a Salvationist had been asked, "What is your church?" the answer certainly would have been "The Salvation Army."

Because of these problems a decision had to be made concerning the sacraments and their place and practice in the Army. The decision was not an easy one nor was it made in the space of days.[16] Booth was torn. On the one side his wife and Railton insisted that the Army cast aside the weight of any ceremony in favor of a full life of faith. On the other side he understood that the sacraments provided meaning in the life of many Christians. Would he be willing to deny this means of blessing to his soldiers? He must decide: "Will it help to our great end? If it will not help, will it hinder?"[17] The issue also provided a distraction from the Army's mission. How was the world out there to be saved while people sat around inside and argued over these issues that had not been resolved in centuries of Church debate?

Booth announced his decision on January 2, 1883, at an officer's councils in London:

> I think that you will perceive that any order from me for the general administration of the sacraments would likely produce grave dissensions. . . . If the introduction of them would create division of opinion and heart–burning . . . I cannot accept any obligation as binding upon my conscience, neither will I seek to bind any upon yours, to do, to believe, or teach anything for which authority cannot be furnished from the Word of God, or which God Himself does not reveal to us by His Spirit, as our present duty.[18]

The turning point had been reached—The Salvation Army would discontinue the observance of the sacraments.

Defending his actions, Booth reminded the officers that a ceremony could only represent a greater truth. "When a husband goes to America and leaves his wife behind, then his photograph which she has in remembrance is precious to her; she has it on her work table by day and under her pillow at night. But when he returns she throws away the picture or gives it to the child to play with, and she embraces the husband. . . . the Holy Ghost has come; and now that you have Him—the substance—the picture has lost its charm."[19]

Formal reasons for abandoning each ceremony were given. For baptism, the reasons were the following:

1. The all–important baptism in the New Testament was not water baptism but the baptism of the Holy Ghost.

2. Because Jesus Himself never baptized anyone, His example proves it is not essential.

3. The efficacy of the act. The record of Scripture indicates that baptism is not essential to salvation.

4. Conflicting views related to administration.[20]

Reasons for discontinuing communion were as follows:

1. The Lord's example at the Last Supper was meant to call His followers to remembrance at every meal, not just a special observance.

2. Because so much controversy surrounded the observation of communion, it ought to be avoided altogether.

3. As with baptism, it is not essential to salvation nor in itself capable of rendering change in an individual's life.

4. That other commands, such as foot washing, have largely been ignored. That being the case, why should communion receive special attention?

5. The use of wine in communion was a snare to those who had just been saved from strong drink.[21]

Lingering Doubts

Having made the decision, Booth moved on. In uncharacteristic fashion he expressed doubts as to whether his decision was correct. He allowed that, should a soldier feel strongly enough, he would be able to partake in communion or baptism without fear of repercussions.[22] Neither did he feel that the decision was necessarily a once and for all stance for the Army to take. He left the question open for future generations: "Is it not wise for us to postpone any settlement of the question, to leave it over to some future day, when we shall have more light, and see more clearly our way before us?"[23] Although it may have lingered in the Founder's mind, it was officially off limits for discussion. *The Salvation Army Year Book* (1906) voiced the following official position:

> The Army abstains entirely from the administration of any sacrament, and from any speaking or writing on the subject. It recommends each individual to be fully persuaded in his own mind as to his duty, and that those who desire to use this or that sacrament should do so without condemning others who do not. Working alike in Protestant, Catholic and heathen countries, the Army could not possibly take this or that side in these matters, but desires to avoid all controver-

sies or scandals tending to obscure the view of its one great object, the salvation of all, no matter how brought out, who are living in sin and darkness.[24]

Commissioner A. G. Cunningham, former Chief of the Staff and second-in-command of the international Salvation Army, wrote the first article on the subject of the sacraments in the *Staff Review*, May 1929. He repeated much of the same information that had been given originally and the reminder, "It has hitherto been our consistent policy as an organization to abstain not only from the practice of what are commonly known as sacraments, but from any public discussion of the subject."[25] Curiously, however, no edition of *Orders and Regulations* at any level ever prohibited officers from administering the sacraments and no statement is made about them in the *Articles of War—A Soldier's Covenant,* the document every recruit must sign to become a soldier in the Army.

Perhaps conditioned by past departures from the established norm, Salvationists raised little objection to the change. Their hearts were set on the salvation of the world and were likely to be relieved to have one less thing to worry about. It also strengthened their argument with the unchurched that the Army was something different. It would not be so easily swept aside by attacks leveled against the Church at large.

Embracing a New Symbolism

In reality, it was not that The Salvation Army cast aside ceremony so much as it was that it substituted its own ritual. Infants were no longer baptized; they were dedicated, a practice adapted to underscore that no grace was conferred upon the child through the ceremony. The ceremony challenged parents to raise the child in a Christian home, train him to be a Salvation soldier and to be compelling examples of holy living. The parents were not to see themselves as trustees as much as caregivers. The words of the dedication service from the 1906 edition of *Covenant Services* reveals this outlook:

> If you wish the Lord so to take possession of the soul and body of this child that it shall only and always do His will, you must be willing that it should spend all its life in the salvation war, wherever God may choose to send it; that it should be despised, hated, cursed, beaten, kicked, imprisoned, or killed for Christ's sake.

You must let it see in you an example of what a Salvation
Army soldier ought to be, and teach and train it to the best
of your ability to be a faithful soldier, giving all the time,
strength, ability, and money possible, to help the war.

You must keep as far from the child as you can all intoxicat-
ing drink, tobacco, finery, wealth, hurtful reading, worldly
acquaintance, and every influence likely to injure it, either in
soul or body; and you must carry out, to the best of your ability, the will of God, and the wishes of your superior officers
with respect to it.[26]

The public enrollment of senior soldiers became a ceremony of testimony. Required to sign the *Articles of War,* recruits claim a personal
experience of salvation, adherence to Salvation Army doctrine, a holy
lifestyle that includes abstinence from alcohol and other harmful sub-
stances, unworthy reading material and any other influence that might
harm themselves or their witness. They further pledge to support the
Army and to remain faithful to it. In a more detailed ritual, soldier enrollment more closely parallels the strong claims of adult baptism.

The Love Feast provides a parallel to communion. It differs in that the
Love Feast does not claim to offer any means of grace, nor are the elements
representative of the body or blood of Christ. No one fills a priestly role.
Characteristically using water instead of grape juice and crackers or bread
in place of unleavened bread or communion wafers, the emphasis tends
to be upon the spiritual life of the corps body providing an opportunity
for reconciliation and mutual prayer. The Love Feast could be highly
sacramental in feel if not in practice. No set ritual was ever put in place.

A Century of Questions

That these ceremonies have taken on such potent meaning reminds
Salvationists that people continue to need symbolism. Beyond the ceremonies the Army was full of symbolism—from the flag, to the uniforms,
to the colorful language. William Heathcote marveled,

The whole character and nature of the Army, all its methods
of action, would lead one to expect that it would be strongly
sacramental. To anyone who understands the nature of the
movement, it must come as a surprise that the leaders do not
lay stress on sacraments. They lean much upon externals

and ritualism; they believe tremendously in their place and position; one would expect them to go on to sacraments. . . . How is it then possible that they should fail to grasp the idea of the sacraments, and not readily see that God, wishing to convey Himself to us, graciously condescends to treat us as men with bodies as well as spirits, and gives us earthly material sacraments, whereby to convey heavenly grace? . . . In absolute and manifest contradiction to their whole character and nature, they abandon the sacraments altogether.[27]

That the Army's position on the sacraments has been in place for over a hundred years has not ended the discussion. In 1998 the International Spiritual Life Commission, called by General Paul Rader, met to discuss several issues, including the sacraments. After considerable discussion, the commission essentially confirmed the Army's traditional stance. It did, however, suggest the increased observance of "the fellowship meal" as outlined below.

Recognizing that every meal may be hallowed, whether in the home or with the congregation, there are strategic occasions when the planning of a fellowship meal may especially enrich corporate spiritual life. Such occasions could include the following:

- In preparation for and during the Easter period.

- At the beginning of a mission or spiritual campaign.

- At a corps celebration (e.g., an anniversary, a New Year's watchnight service, the opening of a new building).

- At a soldiers' meeting.

- For the census board or corps council, particularly when important decisions need to be made.

- For the launching of the Annual Appeal when the significance of work/service undertaken in Christ's name could be emphasized.

- Harvest/Thanksgiving.

- Between meetings when a meal is required and members

of the congregation are unable to travel home to eat because of distance.

- When there has been a breakdown in relationships and healing is sought by reflecting on Christ's great act of reconciliation through the Cross.

- Whenever it is thought that such a gathering would strengthen the spiritual life and wider fellowship of the corps or center.

- Small group meetings, especially house groups, mid–week meetings or (for example) at the conclusion of a recruits' preparation for soldiership course.

- Corps camps, fellowship weekends, or retreats.

Although the fellowship meal is suggested for almost any occasion, there is no information as to exactly what is meant by a fellowship meal. Perhaps the commission chose to leave this open ended in order to resist even a hint of formalized sacrament. However, it did remind Salvationists of the traditional Army position:

> We call Salvationists worldwide to rejoice in our freedom to celebrate Christ's real presence at all our meals and in all our meetings, and to seize the opportunity to explore in our life together the significance of the simple meals shared by Jesus and His friends and the first Christians.[28]

This issue remains resistant to easy solutions. No longer is there a problem with women in ministry. The use of nonalcoholic grape juice has become a part of many Protestant communion services. The Army's distinctiveness as a religious body apart from the churches is not as apparent as it once was. Yet, there is some strong argument for keeping to the nonsacramental stance.

Placing trust in ceremonies over experience remains a problem for some people. In many countries where the culture has included rituals that carried the idea of magical powers, the meaning of the sacraments can be easily confused. After centuries of teaching in the Western world there are still many hundreds of thousands who have trusted in a ceremony instead of the Savior. Why should it be expected that it would be less confusing for those first–generation Christians in lands where superstition was a part of everyday existence?

However, in other places, while it is recognized that there is no "magic" in the sacraments themselves, there is significance beyond doing the ceremony for ceremony's sake. In Asia, many families who are non–Christian do not object to family members attending a church. Some do not even mind it when they claim a salvation experience. But the signal to the world that they are forever turning their backs on the old gods and religions is public baptism. This is a statement that once and for all they are finished with the old ways. So the questions in Asian countries would be "Are you a Christian?" meaning, have you decided for Christ? Then, "Have you been baptized?" meaning, have you decided to turn from the old religions and hold to Christianity alone? The Salvation Army stance, then, is a problem because joining the Army as a soldier may not appear in some cultures to be as strong a statement as submitting to public baptism.

Faithful to Essentials

It is also worthy to note that a number of denominations have in the past century drifted toward liberalism. In that drift the inspiration and authority of the Scriptures has been compromised, as well as the unique place of Christ as fully God and fully man, and the need for Christians to live pure lives in the world. Though these essentials have been abandoned, the ritual of the sacraments remains intact. The Bible echoes the voices of the ancient prophets as they decry Israel's slavish devotion to ritual while abandoning true devotion. For this reason, it is naive for The Salvation Army to suppose that adding the sacraments will necessarily add to the quality of its spiritual life. The life of the Christian remains one of faith and relationship with God. If the heart is not right, there is no ceremony that can change that. If the sacraments were restored tomorrow, they would not in themselves signal another Pentecost. By way of example, both the American Rescue Workers and the Volunteers of America (see Chapter 2) added the sacraments. Sacraments have provided no safeguards to their spiritual vitality.

On the other hand, no issue over the years has put Salvationists on the defensive more than this one. It remains the single most difficult issue to explain and to understand.

In 1974 the World Council of Churches presented the Lima Text that outlined common tenets among member churches. They particularly emphasized baptism and the Lord's Supper as being essential to the Christian faith. Challenged by this the Army attempted to answer by restating its belief that sacraments were not a ceremony issue but a lifestyle issue. All of life was to be sacramental.[29]

A more formal response came from the pen of Commissioner Philip Needham, PhD, author and Southern territorial commander. In *Community in Mission: A Salvationist Ecclesiology*, he writes:

> In order for there to be true unity in the (universal) gospel, there must be freedom in the diversity of culturally conditioned forms, rituals, ceremonies and governments in the Church as a whole. The strength of the universal gospel is that "it is the power of God for salvation to everyone who has faith, to the Jew first and also to the Greek" (Romans 1:16). In order to protect this universality, the Church must allow for considerable diversity in the expression and nurture of faith, so that acceptance of the gospel does not depend upon simultaneous acceptance of a particular culture or ecclesiastical tradition and thereby nullify the universality. It is a disservice to the gospel to insist that grace must be received through the mediation of a particular ritual or procedure, and there is no evidence in the New Testament from which a case can be argued for such a view. Grace is immediate and accessible. When the Word became flesh, God's grace appeared for the salvation of all men (Titus 2:11), "and from His fullness have we all received grace upon grace" (John 1:16).[30]

Although the Army has singled out these church traditions for exclusion in its corporate life, it adheres to many others such as congregational singing, the sermon, public prayer, gathering for worship on Sunday and the very shape of its chapels. Whether it chooses to call itself a church or not, the Army cannot divorce itself from the context of the universal Christian Church.

It should also be noted that in Latin America where the culture is heavily influenced by the Roman Catholic Church, the legitimacy of the Army has been questioned over the issue of the sacraments. It is a common experience for their youth to attend the Army, only to leave it later to "join the Church." Something as deeply ingrained in the culture cannot be dismissed easily.

The mixed opinions of Salvationists themselves prove that the question is not yet settled. There are those who resist the addition of the sacraments because it would partially dilute what makes the Army unique and compromise the high ground of salvation by faith alone. But the danger might be that we become traditional in a non–traditional position, not willing to investigate the merits offered by those whose opinions differ. Most Salvationists are somewhere in the middle, perhaps wistful about the ceremonies but too committed to the overall message of the Army to let it drive them away.

In Darkest England

What might happen if The Salvation Army allied itself with the cause of a victimized thirteen–year–old girl? The answer: Great Britain would be shaken. And what would happen if William Booth likened people to horses and London to a diseased jungle? The Island Empire and The Salvation Army would divide into camps and transformation would take place.

William Booth found his destiny in the bleakest area of the world's greatest city. He was moved, not only by the sin that reigned almost unchecked, but also by what the sin did to people. Like Jack the Ripper, who stalked and stole life, sin seduced and then destroyed. And those who found their hope in Christ and forsook sin found that they still dressed in rags and were either unemployed or terribly exploited for their labor. The Salvation Army made some initial attempts to address these problems. But the money was not there to sustain evangelism and food depots. Booth also had a basic distrust for gratuitous charity. Early organized efforts to raise living conditions for the desperate of London were forsaken, though individuals in the Army occasionally reached out as their hearts and means allowed.

Maiden Tribute

William Booth was largely on the sidelines when the Army made its first serious foray into social service. A lone soldier known only as Mrs. Cottrill began a small rescue work in her home for women, many of whom had been lured into prostitution. Booth appointed his daughter–in–law, Bramwell's wife Florence, to oversee this embryonic program. Although the effort was small, the need was immense. Prostitution was an open part of Victorian life, a strange anomaly given society's unwillingness to openly discuss sexual matters. Perhaps it was this reluctance to discuss the issues that allowed promiscuous expressions to continue in the shadows. For far too many girls it was the only trade they had to provide a living. Booth commented, "The profession of a prostitute is the only career in which the maximum income is paid to the newest apprentice."[1]

Although Army leaders had a vague idea of the evils associated with prostitution, they were stunned to discover the hopelessness and help-lessness of women and girls involved. Florence brought home tales of heartbreak and horror to her husband who at first suspected she was exaggerating. Perhaps the girls were manipulating a sympathetic lis-tener in order to receive more help. But Bramwell became a believer when a seventeen–year–old girl waited one morning for the doors to open at International Headquarters. Having come to London in response to an advertisement for a housekeeper, the girl found herself in a broth-el instead. She finally escaped from a locked room in the dead of night and searched for the International Headquarters address inside a small Salvation Army *Song Book.* Investigation confirmed her story.

Florence advised Army leaders that there were many more young girls who made similar reports. The whole sordid truth was beyond denying and now it was impossible to look away. Bramwell was deeply troubled, then incensed and then moved to act.[2]

Realizing he needed an ally, Bramwell went to a trusted friend and prominent newspaper editor, W. T. Stead, and outlined what he had dis-covered. When Stead heard the story, he slammed his fist on the desk in anger.[3] The younger Booth had found a partner. Stead's position as edi-tor of the influential *Pall Mall Gazette* empowered Booth for action.

One of the Army converts in London was a woman named Rebecca Jarrett. She began a life of prostitution at twelve years of age and became a brothel keeper herself. Booth and Stead approached her about helping them prove how easily young girls could be bought and lured into pros-titution. At first she refused. She had left that life of shame and never wanted to look back. But when they prevailed upon her, pleading on behalf of the girls who might be spared the life she had known, she reluctantly agreed to help.

At a park where girls as young as six came with their mothers to be sold into prostitution, Jarrett found the mother of thirteen–year–old Eliza Armstrong. Jarrett paid the mother the agreed–upon sum of money, and the girl was given over to her. After an examination confirmed the girl's health to be good, she was sent to France in the safekeeping of a single woman Salvation Army officer.[4]

It was time for the world to know. On July 6, 1885, Stead ran the first of ten articles under the title "The Maiden Tribute of Modern Babylon." A lightning strike on Parliament could scarcely have created a greater stir. Editions of the paper were sold out. Police were stationed at the newspaper office to keep order as mobs demanded to read about the shame that England had chosen to ignore.[5] Other papers angrily denounced The Salvation Army and the *Pall Mall Gazette* either because they had missed the most sensational story of the year or because they felt that ethics had been breached to produce it.

After the startling disclosures in the *Pall Mall Gazette,* mass meetings were held across London. With passion and eloquence Catherine Booth added her voice in righteous indignation against those in Parliament who sided against the Army:

> I read in some paragraphs from the report of a debate in the House of Commons which made me doubt my eyesight. . . . I did not think we were so low as this—that one member should suggest that the age of these innocents . . . should be reduced to ten and, O my God!, pleaded that it was hard for a man—hard, for a man—having a charge brought against him, not to be able to plead the consent of a child like that.
>
> Well may the higher classes take care of their little girls! Well may they be so careful never to let them go out without efficient protectors. But what is to become of the little girls of the poor? Of the little girls of the working classes? I could not have believed that in this country such a discussion among so–called gentlemen could have taken place.[6]

The Salvation Army helped sponsor a petition urging Parliament to raise the age of consent to eighteen, make the procuring of children for immoral purposes a criminal offense. The petition allowed magistrates power to enter any house where girls were held against their will and an equalizing of the law made it illegal for a man to solicit a woman, even as it was then illegal for a woman to solicit a man.[7] For this petition 393,000 signatures were gathered. The petition was borne on poles by eight Salvation Army cadets to the House of Commons.[8]

The needed legislation passed but with an amendment raising the age of consent to sixteen. Before the victors could enjoy their achievement, an incredible turn of events resulted. W. T. Stead, Bramwell Booth, and Rebecca Jarrett were arrested, the first to be charged under the new law. Enemies in the press had succeeded in slamming the Army and their editorial rival in one fell blow. As the trial began for the three, Rebecca Jarrett cracked under the strain, resulting in a short imprisonment. Bramwell Booth was acquitted completely. W. T. Stead spent three months in jail; an imprisonment his journalist's heart savored.

Although the whole undertaking had been colored by the fiasco at the end, the Army learned something about itself. Championing the right cause, it could make a difference for the oppressed. It was a lesson that would never be forgotten.

Growing Involvement

During the next five years the Army slowly added shelters and other services for the poor. During a crisis in 1888 a shelter was opened in Limehouse where meals were sold for a penny, supper and a night's lodging for three pence.[9] Not only were Salvationists working to meet some critical needs but they were also gathering first hand knowledge about the plight of London's poor. It was the only way to gather information. As Booth noted with disgust, it was easier to find books on earthworms than on the poor.[10] It wasn't as if these conditions were hidden from sight. In London's East End one privy could serve up to forty people with piped water available but one hour a day. Overcrowding forced as many as six to eight people to share a single bed.[11]

An apt description is shared by historian Barbara W. Tuchman:

> . . . the poor, where hunger and dirt were king, where consumptives coughed and the air was thick with the smell of latrines, boiling cabbage and stale beer, where babies wailed and couples screamed in sudden quarrels, where roofs leaked and unmended windows let in the cold blasts of winter, where privacy was unimaginable, where men, women and grandparents and children lived together, eating, sleeping, fornicating, defecating, sickening and dying in one room, where a teakettle served as a wash boiler between meals, old boxes served as chairs, heaps of fowl

straw for beds, and boards propped between two crates as tables, where sometimes not all the children in a family could go out at one time because there were not enough clothes to go around, where decent families lived among drunkards, wife–beaters, thieves and prostitutes, where life was a see–saw of unemployment and endless toil, where a cigar–maker and his wife earning thirteen cents an hour worked seventeen hour days seven days a week to support themselves and their children, where death was the only exit and the only extravagance and the scraped savings of a lifetime would be squandered on a funeral coach with flowers and a parade of mourners to ensure against anonymity and the last ignominy of Potter's Field.[12]

Reaching the Suffering

Scattered efforts were made to reach those who were suffering. But as the Army grew more and more involved in helping the oppressed, Booth began to formulate a bold comprehensive plan. The framework for its unveiling came, not from the kind of publicity that served so well in the Maiden Tribute Campaign, but from a celebrated African explorer.

Sir Henry Morton Stanley, explorer, writer, and empire builder, had recently returned from an expedition to central Africa in search of the missionary Dr. David Livingstone. In *In Darkest Africa,* his best–selling two–volume book published in 1890, Stanley described scenes of cannibals and pygmies, of vicious jungle life, and the devastating toll of disease. The British people were fascinated by these dangerous, exotic tales.

Taking Stanley's adventure as his cue, William Booth countered with his own tale of savagery and viciousness:

> As there is a darkest Africa is there not also a darkest England? Civilization, which can breed its own barbarians, does it not also breed its own pygmies? May we not find a parallel at our own doors and discover within a stone's throw of our cathedrals and palaces similar horrors to those which Stanley has found existing in the great Equatorial forest? . . . How strange it is that so much interest should be excited by a narrative of human squalor and human heroism in a distant continent, while greater squalor and heroism not less magnificent may be observed at our very doors.[13]

This concept became the premise for his own book, *In Darkest England and the Way Out.* The scheme proposed was admittedly nothing new.[14] In fact, in the appendix he cited a similar successful social experience in Bavaria a century earlier.[15] The originality of the *Darkest England* scheme was not the issue; it was society's reluctance to deal with the problem it revealed.

Commissioner Frank Smith, head of the Social Wing that carried on the Army's humanitarian work, wrote, "If governments, communities, and individuals fail to recognize their responsibilities, The Salvation Army must lead the way, and stepping into the breach, throw its energy into the struggle for the temporal as well as the spiritual salvation of the people."[16] Interestingly, fellow Londoner Karl Marx, in collaborating with Friedrich Engels a few years earlier about these same social ills, formulated a theory that served as the basis for communism. But there is a fundamental difference between the two views. Communism decreed that the world could be changed by denying God; Booth insisted it could be done only with God's help.

William Booth made his case first to the public. After the initial allusion to Stanley's book, he outlined the need. Referencing information from various published sources, interviews, and the Army's own experience, he estimated that ten percent of England's population were those "who have gone under, who have lost their foothold in Society." They were "those to whom the prayer to our Heavenly Father, 'Give us day by day our daily bread,' [was] either unfulfilled, or only fulfilled by the Devil's agency: by the earnings of vice, the proceeds of crime, or the contribution enforced by the threat of law."[17] He would refer to this estimated ten percent of the population as the Submerged Tenth. According to the standards Booth had set, one third lived in the city of London alone. They numbered around three million people, roughly the population of Scotland. He pleaded that a standard of decency should be set, and called it The Cab Horse Charter.

He reminded his readers that when one of the horses that commonly pulled wagons and carts through city streets fell to the ground it was immediately helped to its feet, regardless of the cause of the animal's fall. This was done not only out of pity for the horse but in order to unsnarl the traffic impeded by the fall. Secondly, the cab horses could be assured of a shelter for the night along with food and work to earn its keep. Thirdly, it was the law to help the horse. If we can make such basic provisions for common work animals, Booth proposed, could there not be at least this same standard for human beings, who were possessors of eternal souls?[18]

He identified the people who were in need and the problems each group uniquely presented. The list included the homeless, the unemployed, those who were living a hand–to–mouth existence, those sustained by criminal activities such as prostitution and thievery, criminals and children whom he lamented with Bishop South, were "not so much born into the world as damned into it."[19] Attacks were launched against the sweatshops, brothel keepers, publicans (bar owners), and those who produced and promoted alcohol. He also condemned the government's woeful provisions that more frequently worsened the problems rather than providing solutions. Nor was he impressed with what was being done by some social agencies that failed to provide a long–term hope: "It is no doubt better than nothing to take the individual and feed him for a day or two, to bandage up his wounds, and heal his diseases; but you may go on doing that forever, if you do not do more than that; and the worst of it is that all authorities agree that if you only do that you will probably increase the evil with which you are attempting to deal, and that you had better let the whole thing alone."[20]

Three–Tier Colonies

The main framework of the plan included three components: the City Colony, the Farm Colony, and the Overseas Colony. The City Colony would put the Army in direct contact with the Submerged Tenth. The programs offered would be the entry point for those in need, with the most pressing needs such as food and clothing to be addressed first. The poor would be immediately set to work and brought under the Army's religious teaching. Booth was very clear in his insistence that spiritual influence was fundamental to rehabilitating any person. "I propose to go straight for these sinking classes, and in doing so shall continue to aim at the heart. If we help the man it is in order that we may change him."[21] It was expected that some would find permanent employment or be taken in by family members, thus requiring no further service.

Booth felt that the city was not only a place where sin was found, but it was itself evil. The sooner a person could be taken out of the city the better off he was likely to be. He described an individual lost in the city as "a mere human ant, crawling along the granite pavement of a great urban ants nest, with an unnaturally developed nervous system and a sickly constitution."[22] Ironically, except for occasional holidays, William Booth was a lifelong city dweller.

If a person proceeded through the City Colony and other suitable arrangements were not made, he could then be promoted to the next level, the Farm Colony. The Farm Colony was envisioned as an estate not too far distant from the city where the religious training and nurturing would continue. The colonists would be taught farming skills, offering options over city life or preparation for life in other lands, should they choose to emigrate.

Booth expected that farm life would not only provide employment and learning opportunities but benefits and other merits would make country life desirable over city life. Once again, it was hoped that some people might then be returned to families or join a farmer in a rural setting. Still others would be given the chance to graduate to the next level—the Overseas Colony.

Booth saw in the British colonies untold opportunities for those who had proven themselves. A person could start over in a new place where opportunities were limited only by the breadth of one's ambition. He cited the millions of available acreage in South Africa, Canada, and Australia. These colonies would welcome rehabilitated people, who could secure a tract of land and begin anew. The Army would provide supervision and support while the immigrants went through a period of adjustment.

Getting to Work

Booth laid out the ambitious plan. "Why not?" he asked.[23] *In Darkest England and The Way Out* was completed while Catherine Booth was dying of cancer and released in November 1890. Although Catherine often spoke with her husband about the ideas and plans for the book, she would not live long enough to see it launched. To his credit, Booth pushed on, perhaps welcoming some distraction from his grief over her death. It was a grief from which he would never fully recover.

The book sold out its run of 10,000 copies on the first day. Reaction was swift. Praise for the plan included that of nineteenth century author, journalist, and magazine editor, Sir Wilfred Meynell:

> I rise from the reading of it . . . with a strong impression that
> here is a proposal which they who will not bless it do well
> to abstain from banning. Here is at last a man who has for-
> mulated a comprehensive scheme, and has dared to take
> upon himself its execution. Here was this vast putrescence
> at our very doors, and what scavengers of charity might
> endeavor its removal? Now comes by a man and offers to
> take on himself the responsibility of that removal. In God's
> name, give him the contract![24]

An enthusiastic songwriter put it down in verse:

> *When a cab horse falls upon the street,*
> *No matter who's to blame,*
> *If carelessly he missed his feet,*
> *They lift him just the same.*
> *The sunken of our fallen race,*
> *A tenth is not a few,*
> *We'll lift them up in every case,*
> *When the General's dream comes true.*
>
> from *Combat Songs of The Salvation Army*

A Dangerous Radical?

Others were frightened by Booth's proposal. A typical reaction in
this vein was published in the *Atlanta Constitution:*

> If General Booth is like ordinary mortals he is the most dan-
> gerous reformer that has appeared in the present century.
> How long will he and his followers be satisfied with volun-
> tary contributions? When they realize their power they will
> increase their demands. It will not be strange if they finally
> resort to violent methods to distribute poverty on a more
> equal scale. In the name of religion and reform blood has
> been shed in the past, and history may repeat itself.[25]

Later attacks would prove more devastating, such as the one delivered by a sworn enemy of William Booth, Professor Aldous Huxley, the
most famous atheist of the nineteenth century. His attacks on William
Booth and The Salvation Army in the "Letters to the Editor" section of the

London Times probably did more to dissuade support for the plan than any other single deterrent. Other critics included former Salvation Army commissioner Alex Nicol, who wrote, "[The Army] has attacked many, but solved no single problem. It has drawn into its many nets of mercy thousands of the ghosts of our social underworld and inspired them with cheer and some little hope; but the march of poverty still goes on."[26]

Those who rendered such judgments misunderstood Booth's intentions. At no time did he claim he had the once–and–for–all solution to the world's poverty. As one of his biographers wrote, "He made no claim to inaugurating a millennium. He was too sensible, too practical, too experienced, too well–informed to believe he could so change all human nature as to wash the land clean of crime, vice, and poverty."[27] In fact, it was because he was so aware of human nature that he assumed the Army would never run out of work once the task was begun.

Partial Success

The largest problems involved in executing the plan's initiatives were old ones—finances and personnel. Booth asked for £100,000 to initiate the plan and an additional £30,000 per year to keep it operating. He was successful in raising the amount for the first year but failed in subsequent years. In spite of that shortfall, he was able to establish a wide array of services in the city and to start several farm colonies. Overseas colonies did not come about as he planned, but shiploads of emigrants made their way to new lands under Salvation Army direction. While not a total success, the Darkest England plan was enough to inspire the confidence of those who supported the Army.

The plan was exported to other countries, most notably the United States, where it may have rescued the Army from complete ruin following the resignation of Ballington and Maud Booth. The Army there poured its energies into this new plan. A public angry over what it perceived as ill treatment of the Ballington Booths now rallied behind this effort to do something about the growing poverty found in American cities. In the late 1890s the survival of the Army in America was far from assured. The social work scheme internally gave the Army a new sense of direction while it engaged the American public to support its efforts.

The cry for personnel was partially answered. Booth chose to separate the religious and social branches for the sake of accountability.

Officers who served in one could not serve in the other. Balance had to be maintained between the twin advances of the religious and social work. In the United States the plan was modified by then National Commander Commissioner Frederick Booth–Tucker to include some separation of social work from corps work, most notably the Men's Social and the Women's Social programs. But largely the social work was incorporated into the overall framework of a corps. It worked, and created a Salvation Army in the United States that is so tightly joined that the spiritual and social work form one entity.

Organizational Change

Booth's heart was set on doing something about the plight of the poor. It is unlikely that he anticipated how dramatically the *Darkest England* scheme would change the Army. After first combining the military and ecclesiastical structure, the Army then distinguished itself by creating an organization that was fully a Christian denomination and fully a social service agency.

Other effects resulted from the added component of social work. The Salvation Army was increasingly viewed as more than a band of religious eccentrics; it was seen as a force for good. So thoroughly has this impression been created in the minds of people that the Army is often looked to for solutions when none seems apparent. The amazing efficiency and practicality of its social work has created a legacy of public trust.

Because the Army has consistently reached those in the deepest need with meaningful services, it has been seen as a beacon for the poor. In 1904 when William Booth addressed officers in council he said, "The Salvation Army stands for hope; that, when every other light is extinguished, and every other star has gone down, this one gleam shines steadily and clearly out in the darkened sky: 'If I could only get to The Salvation Army, they will do something for me.'"[28]

This heritage of hope has paved the way for myriad social service organizations serving a variety of human need. The Army proved that the needs of people could be met and, when presented to the public in the proper way, they would respond with compassion. Social work also raised public awareness for the Army and its varied programs, and gave it a wider sphere of influence.

Providing social services has had its costs as well. The work of the Army is often splintered between that which is predominantly spiritual and that which is social. In the United States, an officer can be frustrated in attempts to meet the physical needs of his city while also trying to meet the spiritual need of his corps. This too often results in the officer becoming only a part–time pastor. During the week he is the administrator of one of the largest social service agencies in town. On the weekend he is the pastor of a congregation that often needs more attention than he may be able to provide with limited help.

In countries where the social and corps work are separated, it is not unusual for each to function independently, with little effort to integrate or even coordinate efforts. This is not difficult to understand. The focus of social services toward the immediate physical and emotional needs differs from the corps' primary focus of the spiritual well–being of its people. These are not mutually exclusive, and quite often deep spiritual needs are met effectively within social services expressions and social service needs met at the corps level. But because the officers and staffs are essentially facing in different directions, they can fail to keep the other in their line of sight.

In addition, where the social work is separated from corps work, there can be a competition for funding and other public support. The public is often willing to fund practical concerns at a higher level than spiritual ones.

The Salvation Army has also found itself occasionally at odds with local governments and neighborhood associations when seeking suitable locations for its properties. Fearing increased crime and decline in property values, or stopped by the specter of the homeless wandering around their streets, some local government leaders have cried, "Not in my backyard!"

Social work efforts sometimes eclipse the spiritual focus of the Army's work. Despite efforts to inform the public of its unique ministry, the media often gives attention to the social work without mentioning the spiritual dimension. This is particularly true when the Army serves in disasters. When Salvationists attempt to conduct their spiritual warfare, they surprise many with the information that The Salvation Army is more than a social service organization. Also, the assumption that persons who attend The Salvation Army are necessarily poor is a narrow interpretation of who and what Salvationists are.

The changes brought about by the Darkest England scheme challenge us to keep a balance while not forsaking the Army birthright.

The First World War

A landmark event occurred in 1914 when Salvationists from around the world gathered for an international congress. General Bramwell Booth, who assumed command of The Salvation Army after William's death in 1912, joyfully surveyed a splendid array of Salvationists with varied faces and uniforms, all marching under the Army flag. Their united songs, prayers and rejoicing in Christ gave evidence that the Army's long–desired goal might be near: that the whole world could be won for Christ. He would receive His redeemed souls and begin His reign on earth. The Army had reasons to believe this reign was imminent.

The idea that war could settle differences between people was no longer believed. "They believed a new war to be morally impossible because 'men have lost some of their former savagery and disregard for life,' and physically impossible because new weapons were too destructive."[1] Western civilization and customs dominated, and the Christian gospel was being spread more rapidly than at any time in history.[2] Recent advances in technology brought motorcars to the streets, electricity into homes and telephone wires crisscrossing the cities. Even the sky had been conquered by the airplane. For many there had never been a better time to live or more reason to believe that the prophesied Millennium, Christ's thousand–year reign on earth, was just around the corner.

It was with this sense that the delegates of the International Congress boarded their ships to sail home. Soon afterward an obscure member of royalty would be assassinated in the Balkans. In a bizarre series of events that were reckless in their progression and inexpressibly tragic in their consequences, Western civilization marched headlong into World War I. Once again technology outpaced tactics, making possible death to fall from the sky, and for mayhem to be mechanized. Battlefields were splashed with poison gas. Shrapnel from monstrous artillery killed the enemy at long distances. Machine gun bullets sliced through regiments.

Tanks rumbled across "No Man's Land." The most advanced civilizations flailed at each other with primitive and senseless barbarism. Europe hemorrhaged with the blood of its youth. In the first five months of the war, Germany lost close to a million men. In a single battle, 300,000 French died in a two–week period. At the Battle of the Somme, over a million men were lost.[3] Talk of the imminent Millennium ceased, replaced by concerns about survival.

Among the war's casualties was The Salvation Army's central driving belief that the world would be saved. Too many died on those battlefields, and when that happened, there was a corresponding loss of purpose.

A World Changed

No event since William Booth began his worldwide procession from East London so changed history as the first World War. At the beginning, kings, czars, and emperors still defined world politics. When the final gun sounded, kingdoms had been toppled. In Russia, the communists sealed their first victory with royal blood. Ancient institutions were scorned and crushed like debris on a battlefield.

The Church found that it had lost its influence. Christianity seemed impotent to halt the hellish annihilation the so–called Christians had instigated in war. While it tried to deliver the world to Christ, it failed to deliver the world from itself. Paul Johnson, eminent British historian and writer, noted, "Among the advanced races, the decline and ultimately the collapse of the religious impulse would leave a huge vacuum. The history of modern times is in great part the history of how that vacuum has been filled."[4]

People looked elsewhere for answers. Sigmund Freud believed that truth could be found in psychiatric analysis; religion was only an illusion. Though not hostile to religion, Albert Einstein proved that the universe operated on a totally different law than had been assumed. The universe could not be defined by absolutes of defined lines or length. Karl Marx's theory of a new form of government had its proof in Russia, despite how distorted Lenin had made it.[5] Previous answers to life's essential questions were challenged by different voices. And if these past certainties were called into question, what else could people hold as beyond doubt?

The armistice that ended hostilities hardly brought peace. Events and decisions from that conflict only led to a more encompassing and destructive war twenty years later. Flushed with their victory in Russia, communists exported their atheistic solution to the rest of the world. A sense of pessimism and cynicism ensued—except toward The Salvation Army. How had this representation of Christianity escaped?

Triumph Amid Tragedy

In a word, the Army triumphed with the doughnut. What started as a simple act of kindness to young soldiers became the symbol of the unadorned compassion of The Salvation Army. While the world looked at the bleakness of trench warfare and saw its definitions of civilization reworked, the Army offered this little doughnut, presented with a smile and a word of comfort. The incongruity of this act amid such institutional cruelty was startling. There are times in a person's life when the darkness seems all-consuming and then someone does something, and hope is reborn. The Army did that for Western civilization in the mud of Belgium and France.

As Evangeline Booth stood at the docks to send off the first American contingent of officers to serve in Europe, she reminded them of the expectations: "You are not going on a pleasure excursion, or going out of sensational curiosity to see how things look, or to test how it feels to be at the front; but you are authorized by a specific commission and with the confidence of your Commander that you can and will do a specific work. Not one of you must fail. It is quite enough, for us to pay your expenses to be a success; we cannot contemplate paying them to be a failure." With a final note of humor she continued, "Anyone failing will be shot."[6] They were issued gas masks, helmets and .45 caliber side arms to protect them while serving, but there is no record of Salvationists ever wearing the masks or even learning how to use their weapons. Frequently they had to scramble for cover during artillery bombardments or strike their tents as the front lines shifted.

Both the danger they faced and the courage they showed can be found in one soldier's memory. With orders to go behind enemy lines, the soldier advanced deep into enemy territory. Upon finding a small French village destroyed by an artillery barrage, he recounted the following:

> (An) incident so clear in my memory as if it happened only yesterday. One which I blush with shame and I (feel) like a dirty dog. I did not mean to harm a woman anywhere, much less two innocent girls making an effort to alleviate hardships of men at war. . . . My commander, Capt. H— asked if

I could do anything about finding out what was up ahead of our main column. This was necessary in order that our men not get in ambush. . . . I carefully cleaned both guns. . . . I carried two in holsters hung from my belt. I carefully chose several boxes of ammunition, slung my rifle, sharpened my knife, checked my field glasses, laid plan with Capt. H. how I should try to save him . . . was given emergency field rations, knowing full well I was on my own and possibly might never return. . . .

From beyond this stone pile (30 ft. high) I could discern a column of smoke rising. I decided that if I could gain the vantage point of the top of the stone pile I might get a better view of surrounding countryside. I considered my chances of reaching [its] top in view of many enemy soldiers who were singly traveling past said stone pile, some at great distance, some close by. I determined to try a surprise attack on what I was sure were enemy soldiers, possibly wounded, left behind at a campfire at the ruins of an old house. I went back to a stream that I had crossed a few hours before, wet my clothes, rolled in the dust to make myself the same color as stones. Then I started the long ascent to the top, tired and perspiring. I dared only rest a moment for fear of detection. After having a good look behind I crawled over to where I could see the enemy campfire. Drew both guns, laid my rifle where it was quickly available, crawled to where I would have a vantage point, raised both guns—had mouth open to command in German—"Behold!"

My enemy was two SALVATION LASSIES, SLEEVES ROLLED UP, HANDS COVERED WITH FLOUR AND DOUGH with kettle boiling. One had just dropped a few raw doughnuts into a kettle of grease. She still stood over the kettle. Both wore the letter "F" on the collar of their uniform. They told me that they were Scandinavian, *Fralsnings Armen*. I was so ashamed I shivered with cold. It was some minutes before I could climb down. It was unnerving to think that I had come so near destroying something so sacred. When I could get down I was too ashamed to speak. . . . I was too ashamed to face two brave girls that must have been in the enemy camp because I had seen German soldiers

retreating past their campfire. [The] enemy had not dis-
turbed them, but me, I was supposed to be friendly but I had
almost killed.[7]

World War I Scout Kogaka P.

In the course of its service during the war, the Army served hundreds
of thousands of doughnuts. The men and women tried to provide the
most humane services, to hold the hands of the dying or to take dictation
of the last letter home to mother or a sweetheart. In a place of wholesale
brutality, the Army offered the touch of tenderness. It would not go unno-
ticed. The boys wrote home about their boredom, their sorrow, their
homesickness, and The Salvation Army. Typical of these letters was one
a young man wrote his mother. He was known only as "Charlie."

> The Salvation Army has given us a small library with some
> very good books in it. Mother, don't you ever refuse the
> Salvation Army your old newspapers anymore. When the
> boys who have been to the front and have experienced the
> hardships that are bound to come with war come back, you
> will hear the Salvation Army workers praised highly and
> they certainly deserve it. . . . The Salvation Army has served
> hot coffee and doughnuts to the boys in the trenches and I've
> had my share of them whenever we took infantry ammuni-
> tion up to the second and third lines and what's more it was
> women who did this. Women who live in barracks and
> shacks and undergo the hardships of a soldier in action just
> to help keep them cheerful. They braved the shells just like
> a man and I never saw one without a smile.[8]

The word from Charlie and others like him was heeded at home. Up
to that point The Salvation Army had been barely tolerated. Now it was
celebrated. Songs were written in tribute, Salvationists were featured on
the covers of national magazines. Contributions began flowing in. The
National Commander, Evangeline Booth, who knew full well how to
exploit an opportunity for Army advancement, used this golden moment
to forge ahead. A national fundraising campaign, never before attempted,
was scheduled for the second week of November 1918. It was eclipsed
when the Armistice was signed November 11. Nonetheless, the effort
went on, and a grateful public oversubscribed to raise one million dollars, an unprecedented goal for a nonprofit organization.

The Army Changed

This sudden popularity represented not only a change in the public view but also the Army's view of itself. This change of self–perception, though initially subtle, would have lasting effect.

The world was no longer the same. The landscapes of Belgium and France were disfigured with trenches crisscrossing like ghastly surgical scars. Germany and the Central Powers were not only defeated but totally humiliated, their economies in utter ruin. Russia was fighting a civil war that would end in a totalitarian government more oppressive than any previous rule. Great Britain and other allied nations had given a generation of young men to a war that seemed insatiable in its appetite for blood. The United States had for the first time emerged as a world power only to retreat to a self–enforced isolation. Beneath it all a seething unrest affected all levels of international, corporate, organizational and personal dynamics.

It has been said that all wars have been fought to protect the status quo but the status quo is inevitably destroyed in every war. The Salvation Army shared the popular belief that life would somehow return to normal after the boys were shipped home. The villages would be rebuilt and the wounds healed. But it was not to be, either for the world or the Army.

The change that ensued is an amazing one to study. While there were no directives from any headquarters heralding a different march and no debates or discussions held at officer's councils or in the local corps, a shift occurred at all levels of Salvation Army life. Some of these changes had begun to develop before the war, but the post–war periods revealed decisive changes. The original difference involved the core conviction that the Army would lead the world to Christ en masse. It was reflected in the Army's songs, literature, architecture, and artwork.

The Salvation Army has always been peculiar in its hymnody. Singing about itself and its mission in the world, the Salvationists have used song to give voice to the Army's most cherished beliefs. Of the songs penned by Salvation Army writers prior to World War I, almost 31 percent dealt with evangelism and witnessing; after 1920 it dropped to less than 14 percent (The Salvation Army *Song Book* [1987]).

Typical of the early songs were such standards as "Marching On" (1879), "Soldiers of Our God, Arise" (1884), "The Day of Victory's Coming" (1892), and "Christ for the Whole Wide World" (1914). After 1920 the songs tended to be more personal and inwardly focused in their tone and content.[9] This change can be attributed to several factors.

In the early days, a large volume of songs were written and published each week in *The War Cry*. Most were wholly forgettable, but aspiring songwriters were motivated. Songwriters, subconsciously accepting that the Army wasn't able to march around the world and lay it at Jesus' feet, chose instead to write about a "world" more easily conquered: the individual. The Army developed music boards, where selections to be published featured fewer songs about world evangelism and more devotional choices.

Another change involved the Army's literature. The many editions of *The War Cry* and the host of languages in which they are written makes a detailed analysis of these periodicals difficult. Perhaps the shift in content is best seen in the *Officer*, a private magazine published at International Headquarters and launched first in 1893. International in focus, it encourages writers from the global Salvation Army to contribute. Because it is for private circulation among officers and is considered the General's own publication, it is perhaps more reflective of Army life than other publications that tell the Army story to the public.

A review of the articles published in 1905, 1913, and 1920 reveals a decided content shift. In 1905, 21 percent of the articles and poems dealt with evangelism and revival; in 1913, that number had dropped to 14 percent; in 1920 it had dropped to 5 percent. The decline continued until these subjects made up but a negligible number of articles published. This could signify either a change in articles submitted or editorial decision, or a combination of factors.

Philosophical changes were noted in the Army's architecture. The Salvation Army owned little property in its early days, in order to remain mobile. A great many early corps were opened with a flourish only to close soon after. This wasn't terribly bothersome to the early leaders. They would simply pull up stakes and try the town again a few months or years later. Owning property would make it much more difficult to admit failure and move personnel elsewhere. Also, the Army didn't want the soldiery in a particular place to become too "churchy," to be worried more about their building than the people who needed to be saved. It was felt that owning a building tended to make people settled, rather than unsettled, about their world.

The Army also owned little property because it couldn't afford to buy it. Property ownership meant mortgages, upkeep and all the rest; there simply wasn't money to do this.

On occasion, however, the Army bought property and, even more rarely, built its own buildings. Pre–war construction reflected the Army's militant view. Corps were constructed to look like fortresses, complete with battlements. The National Headquarters in the United States even had a cannon that fired each day.[10] In photographs of Army buildings right up to World War I, these features are not only prominent but emphasized. After the war, new buildings did not include these distinctive features, and most of the older buildings were given facelifts.

The artwork changed as well. When Prohibition passed in the United States, *The War Cry* featured Uncle Sam, sword in hand, slaying the dragon Alcohol. It was clear how the Army viewed the legislation.

Artwork of pre–World War I often depicted crowds of people from various ethnic backgrounds being rescued or viewing the Army on its onward march. Sometimes people were sinking in a vast, stormy ocean with Salvationists coming to the rescue or in a great ark as clouds brood in the distance. One image pictured a group of people enjoying the Millennium in the New Jerusalem.

After the war the crowds disappeared. Soul–winning scenes were often the focus but instead of crowds, a sole Salvationist dealt with a single anxious soul. Open–air scenes now showed a handful of listeners instead of hundreds. The crowds did not completely disappear but they were largely gone. Advances in photography left less to the fancy of the artist. Images continued to drift from the idea of world evangelism. Magazine covers included mountains and ancient ruins, or famous people or places.

Why did such a change take place? As indicated earlier, the whole world experienced a profound change after the first World War. Prior to the war there was a widespread belief that progress in technology, science and in international relations would bring on Christ's earthly reign in the Millennium. What the Millennium would look like depended on who you talked to.

It was thought that labor unions would pave the way to a secular kind of Millennium as workers became equal with factory owners. Socio–political theorists like Karl Marx were sure that workers would attain more than good pay—they would eventually create new governments that provided "people paradises." The socialists provided their own spin that while democracy was a good start, the Golden Age was theirs to be had with political change.

The Promise of a Millennium

Science made its millennial promise. Charles Darwin's theory of evolution gave skeptics a foundation for ridding the world of superstition and religion. Science saw man evolving higher and higher, growing infinitely more civilized than the barbarian hordes of a few centuries before. Electricity eliminated fear of night. For the Wright brothers and everyone else, the sky was no longer a restraint. Science would change everything for the better.

Internationally the Western world reigned supreme. China had been beaten into submission, Japan forcibly opened, the expanses of Africa and India colonized. The last half of the nineteenth century had provided relative peace. War was a thing of the past and it was thought that men of learning could settle their differences in civilized ways. The Millennium would come because the nations had learned to make war no more.

The Salvation Army joined most of Christianity in believing that recent advances in world evangelism would yield fruits of peace. And the Army in particular thought it had a role in bringing this to pass. *The War Cry* (USA) published a fascinating glimpse of this theology. Writing in 1895 from a 1995 perspective, the writer said,

> When we consider in our times, and appreciate the fact that we are in the very beginning of the glorious Millennium, we have cause to rejoice. . . . It has not been the reconstruction of society and government—the paternal—modeled after Bible times and practiced by General Booth in his early Army—I say it has not been these improvements, although they have helped. The great power, as we are all aware, is the fact that the people are saved and cleansed from all sin by the Blood of Jesus. This is the power that has brought about this reign of unselfishness and love among all the people of the earth. This is the reason why the entire world speaks the same language, and the word "foreigner" is obsolete. . . . It was upon the debris of social ruin that The Salvation Army built up a grander civilization—one that honored and served God. . . . The Lord was with His Army as He promised (Joel 2:11). In the year 1900 A.D. The Salvation Army numbered 20,000 field officers, in 1925 A.D. 200,000, when every city, village, and hamlet had corps in the entire world. Whole cities had been converted. By this time every other subject discussed by newspapers had sunk into insignificance. In 1950 the world was about conquered, and the devil so discouraged that he gave up the fight.[11]

Although the writer used fantasy to make a point, such language underscored the Army's millennial dreams. But by the time World War I ended, all such grand talk had stopped. In the place of post–millennial theology rose the pre–millennial view of Christ's return and reign, a teaching that includes belief in a removal of the saints through an event called the Rapture, followed by a terrible period referred to as the Great Tribulation that would last seven years, just prior to Christ's return to earth to establish His reign of a thousand years. While most Salvationists accept that the pre–millennial view of Christ's return has more biblical merit, when Salvationists truly believed that their witness and their work would hasten the day of Christ's reign on earth, there was more urgency to the work.

The Salvation Army continued to advance and save souls but with a very different mindset than before. The march was more deliberate, more long–term, with an eye to the future. It would not be a *blitzkrieg* stroke at Satan's kingdom but siege warfare. An example of this can be found in the British territory, where the number of recruits and soldiers continued to rise until 1928. The number of "prisoners" (converts), however, revealed the slowed impetus: 1,605 in 1923; 698 in 1928; 483 in 1930. [12]

This was not entirely negative. The Army had tended to give very little attention to long–term development of its people or its programs. Now it saw a need to provide a more nurturing environment, to bring its people along to spiritual maturity. Officer losses due to broken health began to decline. Resignations declined as well. Converts were more apt to stay with the Army than drift away to other churches. The Army was also forming multi–generational corps. Although Salvationists may have had less vision for the world, their confidence in the grace of God to change people never waned. They would be saved by ones rather than by hundreds.

Though the effect of this change was not immediate, it was widespread. It would take almost seventy years for a reawakening of the vision of winning the world for Christ. It would be a vision not initiated on the theological teaching regarding Christ's return, but by the collapse of another world system.

Meanwhile, General Bramwell Booth was deeply grieved that the war had taken place. He longed for it to end so the Army could resume its onward march, back to where it used to be. What he did not see from his office window was that his Army had changed course. Neither he nor the world could go back to the way things had been. In part, his inability to understand led to the next turning point in Salvation Army history.

The First High Council

Writing prophetically, former Salvation Army commissioner Alexander Nicol said in 1910, "The Salvation Army will have to be tested by a new process. The ability of its commanders, and even the benevolence of its motives and the philanthropy of its operations, have already been well–tried, and the gain to the Army itself has compensated it for any temporary check that it has sustained in consequence of these trials. The day must come when its ethical and ecclesiastical position will also be tested. Escape from such a crucible is as unlikely as it is undesirable. The history of all organized endeavors to make a new religious force shows that sooner or later such an ordeal is inevitable."[1] In 1929 the prophecy was fulfilled.

As previously discussed (Chapter 2), the Founder marched in the opposite direction of his times to establish himself as the sole chief of The Salvation Army. This position was made official in the Deed Poll of 1878, the document that legally established The Salvation Army. A few days before Christmas in 1896 William Gladstone, the Prime Minister of Great Britain, asked General William Booth what provisions had been made for the case of a General who was judged mentally incompetent or morally corrupt and had to be replaced. Knowing that the succession of leadership was one of the most critical issues facing any organization, Gladstone admonished Booth when he admitted that no provisions had been made. Through correspondence with his son, Bramwell, the elder Booth began the process of rectifying this oversight. The result was a revision to the original Deed Poll called the Supplementary Deed Poll (1904). Wording for this document provided for the removal of a General who "shall be found lunatic by inquisition or if all the Commissioners of the Salvation Army . . . declare by writing under their hands that they are satisfied that the General is of unsound mind or permanently incapacitated by mental or physical infirmity from the adequate performance of the duties of his office . . . [or] are satisfied that the General is in consequence of bankruptcy or insolvency, dereliction of duty, notorious misconduct or other circumstances unfit to continue to perform the duties of his office." [2]

General Bramwell Booth

When in 1912 the Founder died, or was "promoted to Glory," as the Army puts it, to no one's surprise Bramwell Booth was named the Army's second General. Upon assuming the office, the new General affirmed not only his spiritual authority but also the legal status of both the 1878 Deed Poll and the 1904 Supplementary Deed Poll. In fact, at his acceptance of the office, he explained the necessity for such a document. [3]

Bramwell Booth's preparation for this office began almost from the moment of his birth on March 8, 1856. The oldest of eight children, Bramwell's one attempt at schooling outside the home ended abruptly when he was roughed up by boys who found him an easy target because of his peculiar ways. The incident left him with permanently damaged hearing. In addition, he suffered from rheumatic fever that affected his heart and limited his physical activity. [4] Despite his physical limitations, he had a keen mind. At fifteen, he was in the full employ of the Christian Mission. As early as 1879 he was second only to his parents under The Salvation Army leaders. [5] In 1881, at age twenty–four, he headed senior officers on the headquarters staff with the position of Chief of the Staff, second only to his father in authority. [6]

Nine years later, the elder Booth knew his wife was dying. Catherine, who had endured a long and painful ordeal with breast cancer, had built the Army as surely as her husband had. With her life slipping away, Booth was forced to make a change. Although he had spoken to his son earlier about his desire to name him as his successor, it wasn't until a month before Catherine's death on August 21, 1890, that Bramwell's name was placed in a sealed envelope. The envelope wasn't opened until after William Booth's death in 1912. [7] Presumably, the impending death of his wife forced Booth to change the name of his successor from Catherine to Bramwell.

Edward McKinley, Salvationist and professor of history at Asbury College, wrote that when Bramwell Booth assumed the office, he did so with a "mystical conception" of his position, convinced that his was a sacred trust. [8] The manner in which he held the office of General is reminiscent of British reformer Lord Shaftesbury, who served in the august House of Lords: "He was born with a consciousness in his bones and brain cells of ability to rule and saw no reason to make any concessions of this prescriptive right to anyone. . . . He regarded himself not only responsible to the people, but responsible for them." [9] Elsewhere, historian Paul Johnson describes this view: "They shared avowed beliefs, almost untinged by cynicism, in power–balances and agreed spheres of interest, dynastic marriages, private understandings between sovereigns and gentlemen subject to a common code and in private ownership of territory by legitimate descent." [10] The concept was called *oligarchy*, simply summarized by saying those who were best trained to rule ought to rule. It was not only a place of superiority but of tremendous responsibility. Those so prepared to rule felt that this was beyond negotiation.

Bramwell faced this certainty within his family when his father explained his reasons for choosing him. The young man could no longer exercise his free will in the matter.

> If I name you, you have no alternative but to accept my nomination whatever my own opinion may be as to your unfitness. But you will say—how does this accord with my . . . remark, "I ought to have convictions of my own and make my own choice"—perfectly, because whatever you choose will only help your qualification, seeing that the definite application to any branch of the work will give your mind that power of systematic application which you need. [11]

The pronouncements of the Founder were consistent with the British practice of passing the family fortune or business to the eldest son as a means of holding the estate together. Bramwell was thus groomed and destined to rule, whether he liked it or not.

Bramwell Booth took command in 1912 according to plan. The intuition of the Founder seemed to be rewarded. During Bramwell's administration the Army advanced into twenty–five new countries, nearly doubled the circulation of its periodicals, and increased its officer ranks by nearly fifty percent. Financial support both internally and from the public grew. [12] As both Chief of the Staff and General he organized and reorganized the Army administration worldwide, shaping the structure of the Army that exists almost intact to the present. His father may have been the captain, but Bramwell built the ship. His energies were directed to people as well, granting up to one thousand interviews a year, participating in eighty annual council meetings in addition to one hundred and fifty other meetings.[13] Given the restrictions of his health and the travel limitations of that day, his pace and accomplishments were amazing.

The Family

William Booth had promoted his children to leading positions in the movement, and freely used their skills in the war. Bramwell Booth shared the belief with his family of rulers who "had no doubt of their inborn rights to govern."[14] The consensus was that the General's children possessed a sense of entitlement and ownership of The Salvation Army,[15] a notion encouraged by both Bramwell and his wife Florence. The children were given preferred seating on platforms during special events, ahead of senior and higher ranking officers.[16] *The Salvation Army Year Book* (1915, 1917, and 1918) reported on each of Bramwell Booth's children's appointments and promotions. Officers and soldiers were expected to remove their hats, bow and give special deference to the children.[17] In 1919, Bramwell Booth appointed his wife as the British Commissioner, the largest field of Salvation Army work in the world.[18] All this made one senior officer comment, "The old General [William Booth] lost his family and saved the Army; this man is keeping his family and losing the Army."[19] The nepotism that William Booth had shown may have been acceptable during the halcyon days of Victorian England, but times had changed. What once might have been considered acceptable now seemed intolerable.[20]

But it was the rapid rise through the ranks of the General's oldest daughter, Catherine, which caused the most alarm. An able officer in her own right, Catherine Booth was the unquestioned leader among Bramwell Booth's children. Although she possessed many gifts, it seemed that her promotions were not based so much on merit but on her place within the family. Granted a furlough because of ill health, Lt. Colonel Catherine had no appointment for three years. Upon her return in 1926 at age forty–three, she was immediately promoted to full colonel and appointed head of the Women's Social Work in Britain, displacing the popular Commissioner Adelaide Cox. One year later, Catherine skipped the rank of lt. commissioner and was promoted to full commissioner. It was universally believed among the Army leadership that the aging General was positioning his daughter to replace him in office.[21]

Growing Discontent

Problems within the Bramwell Booth family extended well beyond the issue of his children's advancement. When the General instituted a mandatory retirement age, one of those affected was his brother–in–law, Frederick Booth–Tucker. Booth–Tucker was enraged that at seventy–three, he was forced to retire. He went to see Bramwell Booth, and his complaints against the General were neither fair nor quiet. In 1927 he anonymously wrote an allegory titled "The Two Wise Mice: A Dialogue Concerning the Government of the Army" that was widely circulated within the Army. Comparing the present General with his father and mother, he faulted Bramwell Booth for the promotion of members of his family, his ill treatment of some Army leaders, and the receipt of royalties on *The Life of General William Booth* by Harold Begbie.

Booth–Tucker did not limit himself to the allegory. He joined forces with a mysterious W. L. Atwood of Fort Worth, Texas to further incite resistance to Bramwell Booth. Atwood began publishing a newsletter titled "The International Salvationist." In the newsletter, Atwood complained about the treatment of the American National Commander Evangeline Booth. He called for the autocratic rule of the Army to be eliminated in favor of a democratic form of government, advocated that The Salvation Army in America separate from the international body failing any reform and criticized the General over the issue of his family and their special treatment. Another missive in 1925, circulated anonymously to staff officers, was titled "The Blast of the Trumpet," which, save for the complaint about Evangeline Booth, covered the same ground.

The Commander

But no one was talking more about the perceived ill treatment of Evangeline Booth than Evangeline Booth herself. One of the younger sisters of General Bramwell Booth, Evangeline had commanded the forces of the Army in America since 1904. The United States, having been the home of two disastrous splits, had been a particularly troublesome field for International Headquarters. Americans as a whole were less than respectful of Britain's place as a nineteenth century superpower. The spirit of nationalism sometimes carried over into the Army, and Evangeline Booth herself was fiercely independent and identified with the spirit of America. She had enjoyed being something of a pet to her father who had been heartbroken by the loss of his daughter Emma, through a train accident in 1903 and the defection from the officer ranks of three other children: Ballington, Herbert, and Catherine (the Marechale). He cherished Eva. For the first few years she commanded in America, Eva found her father more than willing to accommodate her. Naturally, she expected that her brother would also.

Evangeline Booth's popularity was further underscored by the Army's service to the American troops during the First World War. As a whole the nation adored her. When her brother failed to match that adulation she was offended.

Bramwell decided to make some administrative changes, further complicating the relationship. Evangeline's position as National Commander would remain but her position would be diminished in order to give more power to the individual territorial commanders. Further, it was decided to create the USA Southern territory, a move that Evangeline Booth stubbornly resisted. Finally, after almost twenty years in the same appointment, Bramwell decided she should farewell to take another appointment elsewhere.[22] Word of this leaked out while General Bramwell Booth was visiting in the United States, creating an uproar in protest.[23] The proposed administrative changes with regard to the National Commander's position were not made (even though Evangeline Booth had implemented the plan she so strongly resisted when she was General), nor was she farewelled. The USA Southern territory was created in spite of her efforts to have it dissolved.[24]

Although these issues passed, Evangeline's feeling that she was being ill-treated by her brother did not. Typical of comments along this line was one to her sister-in-law, Mrs. General Florence Booth, "I have suffered much. As I look back there seems scarcely a week that some fresh wound has been made."[25]

Beginning to express doubts as to the General's mental fitness, Evangeline took up the cause of the reformers, quickly becoming the most outspoken leader.[26] Of all those who shared the belief that the Army system of government must be reformed, Evangeline was best positioned to speak out. She was as close to being invulnerable as her brother, sharing the Booth name and commanding the strongest Army contingent outside of Great Britain. Possessed of an iron will, Evangeline was a formidable enemy and more than that, a deeply offended sister who seemed to remember every slight and to misinterpret almost every action.

Other Voices

Evangeline Booth and Frederick Booth–Tucker were not the only ones speaking out. The General's long time friend and advisor, Colonel George Carpenter, complained to him about the problems being created by his family. Carpenter wrote, "There is a widespread feeling that you show unseemly preference for your family in the life and affairs of the Army."[27] The General promptly farewelled Carpenter to an appointment in Australia he had held twenty years earlier. This move sent a chill throughout the Army, resulting in a growing call for reform.

From his vantage point neither Bramwell Booth nor his family could gauge how poorly matters were going. High ranking officers who had never met were now corresponding with each other regarding the growing crisis, spurred on by Evangeline's letters to the General which she copied to them. The General became more unyielding in his position. There is no reason to believe he wasn't totally sincere in his belief that the office of General was a sacred trust and the appointment of his successor of primary importance to that trust. He felt not so much that he *would* not yield but that he *could* not yield to demands for reform. It is also likely that the intransigence was not free from the view he had of his family's destiny as a kind of Salvation Army royalty.

Although things had been building for several years, events in 1928 intervened to bring everything to a head. Evangeline continued writing, focusing with growing intensity on the suspicion that the General was planning to name one of his children as his successor. She was certain that person was Bramwell's oldest daughter, Catherine. When the General wrote saying that he had no power to change the method for naming a successor, Evangeline also contradicted his position, citing the Deed Pole's own provision for an alternative. She urged him to implement the provision for a gathering of Army leadership in what was termed a "High Council" to elect the General, not as an emergency measure but as the only means available. She continued to underscore the point he had tried to sidestep: the General had the option to appoint his successor *or* choose another means for the General to be selected.[28]

His confidence shaken, Bramwell Booth consulted with Army attorneys concerning the calling of a High Council. He first discussed with them eliminating the provision of the High Council, but upon being advised that this was impossible, he abandoned the idea. But it was too late. Word shot around the world that he was willing to take such measures to protect his prerogative to name his successor.[29] The General's actions known, the opposition solidified and intensified.

Shaken and Sickened

Within two weeks seven active commissioners and two retired commissioners from the British territory and International Headquarters presented a letter to General Bramwell Booth telling him they supported Evangeline Booth's position. Prior to this he had thought there might have been a few malcontents scattered about the world, or that Evangeline might have the American leaders on her side. He still considered that his staff and other leaders were loyal not only to him and his family, but also to all his decisions.[30]

Booth was devastated. His wife later wrote, "This was the burden that from the receipt of this letter in March was pressing upon his heart, and began to rob him of his sleep. . . . From March 1928, night after night he would talk to me for hours during the night and in the early hours of the morning as to what could be done to meet the situation."[31] The call for his resignation started the General's health problems, from which he never recovered.

Booth acted, but not in concert with the tide of opinion which now was running against him. The Army's attorney, William Frost, was called to go with one of the General's sons to a London Turkish bath where they met the General. Frost recalled,

> With one of our managing clerks as a second witness, I attended at the Turkish baths with the form of nomination in my pocket. The General (who was in the course of taking a Turkish bath and was in a dressing gown) filled in a name, a piece of blotting paper was placed over this (so that we, as witnesses, should not see it), the General then signed the document, and we two witnesses signed it. The date was inserted (it was March 14, 1928), I placed the document in the envelope and sealed it down immediately and brought it away with me.[32]

Apparently the General mimicked the actions of his father. He would have to have named his successor prior to this date in case he was killed in an accident or was otherwise incapacitated. Like his father, he had a high degree of confidence in his wife. Prior to this successor being named, he had undoubtedly named her as the next General. But she was feeling the effects of age, as was he. The mantle logically would pass on to the next strongest family member—his daughter Catherine. Given the rapid promotions and the positioning of her at International Headquarters, the name in the envelope now most certainly was hers.[33]

In April the General returned from a trip to Europe suffering from influenza. While at another engagement in Sheffield, England, he showed definite signs of weakness. On April 12, 1928, he left his office at International Headquarters, never to return.[34] He ventured out to dedicate the William Booth Memorial Training College at Denmark Hill in London on May 10. This was his last public appearance. He was ordered to bed by his doctors, and from then on ceased to function as the General.[35] By June, Mrs. General Florence Booth began expressing her fears that the High Council might be called.[36] She also began to act more and more on behalf of the General although she had no legal authority to do so.[37]

At the same time, those in favor of reform discovered that they had more allies than they previously believed. There was also a growing fear that the General might delay debate, forcibly retiring those sympathetic to reform and appointing potential High Council members who would assure him of their personal loyalty.[38]

The summer passed with no encouraging change in the General's position or in his health. Continuing to deteriorate in the autumn months, Bramwell expressed his fears that his illness might strengthen the call for reform. He was diagnosed with neuritis, a painful condition resulting in loss of reflexes and muscle atrophy. He was also said to be suffering from nervous prostration, better known currently as clinical depression. All of this increased his sleeplessness and further hastened his decline.[39]

Concerned about their General but also about the possibility of reform, Army leaders feared Bramwell Booth's imminent death. If he died before any action took place it was doubtful a successor would be motivated to limit his or her term in office. At this point the Chief of the Staff, Commissioner Edward Higgins, became a prime concern. Higgins would not openly state his position, but he remained loyal to General and Mrs. Booth and diligently executed the duties of his office.[40]

Calling the High Council

Finally some of the leading officers in favor of reform approached

Higgins, who was unwilling to initiate any action in calling the High Council. He was, however, willing to receive a petition from the required seven commissioners.[41] Since the General had definitely taken a very serious turn, if the High Council was to be called, it must be called immediately.

The requisition was quickly presented to Higgins, and the call for the High Council went out immediately. Upon the notification of the General and the official calling of the High Council, the nomination of Bramwell's successor was automatically made void.[42]

Higgins had already warned Mrs. Booth that the High Council was going to be called. Stunned by the attack, the Bramwell Booth family chose not to share the news with the General for fear that the shock would kill him. Then, to the surprise of all, the old General began to rally and for the first time it appeared he might recover his health after all. But it was too late. The wheels were in motion and members of the High Council from across the globe were on their way to London to decide the fate of their leader.

In the meantime, the Chief met with the Army's attorney, William Frost. It was Frost's opinion that "in the circumstances that had arisen, the General's highest duty to his Trust was to vacate his office and himself instruct you to convene the High Council for the purpose of receiving his resignation and electing his successor."[43] Although a letter was drafted for the General to sign, neither Frost's advice nor the letter ever reached him. In spite of the encouraging change in his health, Bramwell was too weak to receive the letter or even to be told that the High Council had been called. It wasn't until December 30 as the High Council members were arriving in London that the doctors felt he could be advised of the news.[44]

Those loyal to the General began to rally to his cause. An anonymous member of the High Council published a paper for private circulation among the members. He wrote,

> It may not be out of place to remind some of the members of the High Council of . . . [a] Christian writer [who] attacks democracy as the enemy of God and a true anti–Christ. Revolution—the forcible turning upon all that has been sacred—even though it may be for a plausible purpose—is a greatly different matter to Evolution, the gradual development of inward propensities and principles. King Demos is

generally prepared to vote for the first, duly supported by intrigue, deceit, falsehood and cruelty, quoting: "The highest interests for the Cause!" . . . In their anxiety for what they deem desirable, they have been led into the adaptation of Jesuitical methods.[45]

The General and his family decided to plead their case to the Army at large, which up until this point was almost totally in the dark about what was happening or why. The General appealed to Salvationists in a letter dated January 6 for the January 19, 1929, issue of *The War Cry:*

> I could have understood that the Commissioners might have been asked to consider whether I should continue in office, but the fact that the Council has been called leaves no room for doubt that the Commissioners who requisitioned the Council were influenced by a desire to deprive me of the power which belongs to every General of The Salvation Army, under our Foundation Deed, of appointing, or naming the manner of appointing their successor. Had I been asked to resign, it would have been a very different matter and I should not, on my own account, have much regretted the request. It was in my mind to appoint a Commission to receive the various options, and to co–ordinate and examine their value and practicability, and to discover:
>
> I.   What changes are desired.
>
> II. Whether they could be brought about without endangering the stability of the Army or our methods.

The letter never made it to the public. When the High Council discovered its existence and the plans to publish it they ordered that all copies of the *War Cry* containing the letter be destroyed. In doing so they clearly exceeded their authority. The High Council is empowered solely to elect a General, not to be a ruling council.

It is highly doubtful that Bramwell Booth authored the letter at any rate. By this time, his family was acting on his behalf. It was undoubtedly reviewed by him and sent with his knowledge, but he was far too ill to have written much of anything.

Before the High Council began its deliberations it was decided to send a deputation to see the General and to try to convince him to retire. Among those who were sent was Commissioner Samuel Logan Brengle, who wrote about his visit to a friend in the United States.

> I thought the General might be up and dressed, though fee-
> ble, to meet us, but we found him in bed, feeble, pale, thin,
> tremulous and much wasted in the flesh. I don't think he
> moved any portion of his body while we were present
> except his eyes and his trembling, feeble hand. He received
> us kindly, called us each by name in a low, hesitating voice;
> asked for time to consider his decision, which was readily
> granted, and prayed slowly with and for each of us. As we
> started to go he said, "Brengle, I am sorry you have to share
> in this affair." I kissed his poor, wasted hand, and suspect,
> looked upon him for the last time.

Reflecting on what he had seen, Brengle wrote, "He is certainly unfit at his age and in his helpless condition for his job. If he does not retire and we have to adjudicate, I shall have to vote against him. There is no alternative."[46]

The General did answer the High Council, but again not with the answer they hoped:

> I am bound to ask myself whether I should be justified in
> laying down the Trust committed to me. Such a question
> answers itself. I cannot do so. I have sworn to preserve the
> Trust committed to me. . . . I am advised that, were I to take
> any other course, serious internal controversy would almost
> invariably arise, and further that the work of the Army might
> be interfered with by a lawsuit of the utmost magnitude, I
> am confirmed in the rightness of the decision which I have
> already made.[47]

Considering Frost's comments cited earlier, it is not certain who advised the General that his actions would result in "a lawsuit of the utmost magnitude." Such a comment could be understood to be a thinly veiled threat of litigation later taken by Bramwell Booth and his family.

Once receiving the answer from the General, the High Council began the work it was called upon—but was loathe—to do. The resolution was made and seconded that General Bramwell Booth was to be declared unfit and removed from the office of General. Brengle recalled, "The last vote was not cast till midnight. The silence of a death chamber was there. You could hear men breathing laboredly. Hearts were well nigh breaking. . . . The old order was passing, making way for the new."[48]

The fateful resolution passed, and the next item of business was to elect a new General. As the date for the High Council approached some thought that Evangeline Booth, leader of the reform movement would be elected. She claimed that she was not interested in the position, but that if offered, she would not turn it down. Evangeline could not have been prepared for the results. She was nominated, as was the Chief of the Staff, Edward Higgins. She gave an impassioned oration of fifty–five minutes; Higgins delivered a quiet, reasoned talk of twenty–five. He was elected by the required two–thirds majority on the first ballot in a stunning moral defeat for Evangeline.

To the Courts

The members of the High Council prepared to wrap things up and go home, assuming their work was complete, but before they could do so, they were served legal papers. General Bramwell Booth had sought an injunction against the High Council, nullifying its proceedings and temporarily restoring him as General. In the injunction, Booth claimed that the Deed Poll of 1904 was invalid. As such, the High Council had no authority to act.

The members of the High Council were caught totally by surprise. When vice–president of the High Council, Lt. Commissioner William Haines heard the news he suffered a fatal heart attack. Most of those who had previously supported the General turned against him for taking an action they considered to be unChristian. Addressing the High Council, General–elect Higgins said, "I could never have believed that General Booth could have dealt such a ghastly blow at the Trust passed to him by his predecessor. . . . General Bramwell Booth accepted office 'upon and subject to the terms not only of the said Deed Poll of the 26th July 1904.'"[49] (I quote from his "acceptance of office" document.) Evangeline Booth exclaimed, "Think of it, dragging us into the Courts—our splendid men—our beautiful banner!"[50]

The secular press, which had been following the story from the beginning, found this last development even more sensational than the original story of the Army's revolt. News of it flashed around the world. Salvationists were finding out about the internal workings of their movement not from their officers or headquarters, but from the daily headlines of their local newspapers. A reporter in *John Bull* wrote, "If we had been asked a month or so ago what community in the world was least likely to burst into the flames of rebellion against its government, most of us would have said The Salvation Army. It seemed so drilled and disciplined to obedience, so absorbed in its tasks, so indifferent to the ordinary controversies of the secular world, that anything like a public brawl over its affairs was unthinkable."[51]

A Second Adjudication

The courts ruled the proceedings of the High Council void because the General was not able to defend himself or to have some representative offer arguments to counter the charges against him. On February 13 the High Council met once again. Speaking for the General, who was still too ill to come to the proceedings, were his daughter Catherine, his physicians, and his attorney. After asserting that General Booth would once again be able to take command of the Army in a few months, Commissioner David Lamb asked the reporting doctor if he was aware of the physical demands upon the General. Lamb quoted Bramwell Booth's own description of the demands upon the General and then asked, "Sir, do you think General Booth can do that?" The doctor replied, "Most certainly not. Only a superman could carry such a program. The Army Founder could, but he was one man in a generation."[52]

After the presentations were made the vote was taken again. Once again, Bramwell Booth was adjudicated unfit for office, and Edward Higgins was elected as the Army's third General. However, the saga was not yet over.

Bramwell Booth lapsed from whatever recovery he had begun to show. His heart weakened. It had beat for the Army when the movement was little more than an affair run from his parents' parlor. He had watched it grow, had engineered its progress, given it form and substance while his father gave it vision. It was the greatest shame of all that one who had so influenced The Salvation Army should end his life as a tragic figure. On June 16, 1929, Bramwell Booth slipped quietly away from this life, taking his place once again at the side of his mother and father.

One More Twist

Booth's passing turned out not to be so quiet after all. Originally his will left all properties pertaining to The Salvation Army to his successor in the office of General, as was his duty as a trustee. But after the second adjudication by the High Council, a codicil to his will named his wife Florence, his daughter Catherine, and his attorney, Mr. Sneath, as trustees of the Army's properties. Although the codicil only affected the properties in Great Britain, in effect it gave the persons named control of The Salvation Army. General Higgins would have to go to the three trustees in order to execute the normal business of the Army in Great Britain.

Once again the Army found itself in court with members of the Bramwell Booth family. During the negotiations with the trustees, considerable discussion ensued regarding the unopened envelope naming Bramwell Booth's successor. The trustees first asked that it be opened as a condition to turning over the trusteeship to the Army. Then it was requested that the envelope be kept until the next High Council and opened then. Later, *The War Cry* reported, "The judgment of the Court was clear and simple, and the effect of it is to establish the validity of the 1904 Deed, the validity of General Higgins' appointment as General, and to order the executors of the late General William Bramwell Booth to transfer to the General upon the trusts of the Army all property and funds that became vested in them as executors of the late General."[53] The envelope remained sealed, its contents never openly revealed. Upon the judgment in favor of the Army, the envelope was then burned.

The process of electing the General by the High Council was formalized in The Salvation Army Act of 1931, and remains the means for the appointment of a General to this day.

Finally, The Salvation Army was able to move on. Brengle summarized the new place where the Army stood. "A mighty people, however much they may reverence their fathers, cannot be looking back to a grave forever as though all wisdom was to be stretched forth from the grave to guide their destinies through all future time and among all nations."[54] It was unfortunate that so much pain was needed to enforce this truth.

World War II and Its Aftermath

Although shooting had stopped in November 1918, there was plenty of evidence that World War I was far from over. Like an earthquake that continues to send aftershocks, the whole earth trembled. Europe tried desperately to right itself and heal the gaping wounds. America slipped into a self–deceived isolation vainly hoping that if it looked the other way it would not have to be involved in what was happening in the rest of the world. Whole economies teetered and then collapsed. Newspapers and newsreels showed people with wheelbarrows full of money needed to purchase a loaf of bread. Aided by advances in technology, dictators more brutal and vicious than history had ever before seen wreaked misery and destruction upon millions. Perhaps it was inevitable that a world so unsettled would seek to find resolution through yet one more suicide attempt.

The first evidence of a new war's brutality came from China, where the Japanese decided to wrestle that great behemoth of Asia. Not content to limit itself to the battlefield against opposing armies, the Japanese committed widespread atrocities against the civilian population. That model would be repeated when the Germans unleashed their lightning war in Europe. The Allies responded in kind with widespread bombings of German and Japanese centers of industry to destroy the infrastructure for the production and delivery of troops and munitions. It was total war on a truly global scale. Even civilians found themselves in the line of fire. If World War I left behind the lingering memory of the blighted battlefields of Europe, World War II left the entire world a battlefield. Death rode the high seas, filled the night sky, and marched its tanks and troops full speed ahead.[1]

Having learned its lessons from the previous war, The Salvation Army mobilized again. There were bandages to prepare, coffee and doughnuts to be served, words of comfort and cheer to be shared. The

Army would serve the troops again, but modified their methods for a war not marked by static lines as in the previous one. Ever resourceful, Salvationists cheerfully pitched in and did what was required. Because the Army had been most prominent in its service among the nations represented by the Allies, it found itself in a position of strength. As the war drew to its conclusion, The Salvation Army's unstained reputation for doing good during a very bad time was sustained.

Oppressed

But as the previous war had proven, The Salvation Army did not escape the war unscathed. Effects both immediate and long–term marked a turning point in Salvation Army history.

After 1937 Salvation Army activities were increasingly limited in Germany. Collections were forbidden, including sale of *Der Kriegsruf* (*The War Cry*). Because of the highly militaristic state of the country, Salvation Army ranks and symbols were banned. The Army lost substantial numbers of officers, soldiers and properties. By war's end, thirty–three of eighty corps properties were destroyed with another eight heavily damaged.[2] The ban that Germany imposed was then extended throughout Europe to those countries under Nazi control. As in Germany, officers and soldiers were taken away by the military needs of the occupying power or were casualties of war. Bombs often demolished Army properties. In Italy, the Army was banned altogether, all meetings forbidden, and its assets confiscated by the government.[3]

As bad as the suffering was in Europe, it was more severe in Asia. In Japan, The Salvation Army was dissolved, and those who even mentioned its name were punished.[4] In the Philippines, Malaysia, Indonesia, China, Korea, Singapore, and other countries under Japanese control, expatriate and national officers were imprisoned while hundreds of Salvationists disappeared without a trace.[5] As the years progressed and violence increased between nations and in civil wars, the pattern was repeated—Salvationists lost, their final destinies hidden. No one knows how many died specifically because of their Christian witness or because of their heroism in the face of certain death.

General Frederick Coutts summed up the immediate effect of the war: "As there was no country in any continent which had not been affected to some extent by the Second World War, so there was no Salvation Army operation which was not in need of reinforcement or replacement or repair. Important still was its manning—especially when it is remembered that every level of Army active leadership was, and is, a determining factor."[6]

Forced Out

When the war ended in 1945, the Army moved immediately to restore its organizational structure and to send reinforcements to the most blighted countries. Its problems were only just beginning. For the first time in its history, The Salvation Army was forced into retreat.

The Army had faced its first forcible exit from a country when the communists gained control of the Russian government. Russia had especially suffered during the war and was determined not to be victimized again. Carrying out their ideal of worldwide communist domination, Eastern Europe formed the Soviet Bloc, a variety of puppet governments under Soviet control. The communist leaders of these governments found The Salvation Army a nuisance best eliminated.

Following the Japanese occupation, the Army in China gathered the remnants of their forces and moved forward again. Their efforts were short–lived, however, as China sided with the communists, and the Army was shut down once more. A few years later during the Korean War, the wearing of uniforms in Korea was banned and Salvation Army properties were sold. Territorial headquarters in Seoul was rented room by room after the North Koreans took almost total control of the peninsula.[7]

Like its experience in other parts of Eastern Europe, the Army in Czechoslovakia suffered loss as well. After it was liberated from Nazi rule, it had but eight corps remaining. But it had survived. It wasn't long, however, until the Army was closed by the communists, citing "security ground(s)."[8] Coutts wrote:

> In the uneasy peace which had followed the first World War the Army flag had been unfurled in Latvia and Estonia as well as Hungary and Yugoslavia. The Russian occupation of Latvia put an end to the work in 1940, though there was a short flicker of life when the German forces briefly gained the upper hand in 1941—but the end came two years later. The suppression of the Army in Estonia [spelled the end of] the work in the two Baltic republics. The year 1950 marked the beginning of the end in Hungary, and the little that was left of the Army's work in that land was attached to Czechoslovakia.[9]

Birth Pangs

The Salvation Army also found itself affected by the political changes in the emerging countries of the world. It was apparent following the first World War that the spread of colonialism was over. World War II proved that the European powers could not protect, let alone govern, their far–flung empires. The people of those colonies, many times aided by opportunistic communists, became more restive. European nations were trying to piece themselves together, and the peoples yearned for their own liberty. This was the time to free themselves. Colonialism was not only out of fashion, but was unravelling at an alarming rate. Very few of the former colonies were in the least prepared for self–government. Coalitions that had been united against the colonial powers were now at odds with each other over which one had the right to rule the new countries.

India proved a sad example of this chaos. Under the leadership of Mahatma Gandhi, the great sub–continent had been campaigning for independence for over a generation. When independence finally came, euphoria was replaced by violent ethnic war. Battles between Hindus and Muslims raged in the streets, as each seemed possessed of an unquenchable thirst for blood. The new country split in two, the Hindu–dominated India and the Islamic nation of East and West Pakistan. But even this agreed partitioning was accompanied by violence, as refugees of the minority religions attacked and pursued each other. The Army's McRobert Hospital was within twenty miles of the new frontier and found itself overwhelmed with casualties from both sides of the conflict.[10]

The experience of Zimbabwe (formerly Rhodesia) provides an example of the difficulties faced in the new nations of Africa. The minority white government attempted to keep things as they had been under British rule. But the Africans remembered that this had been their land long before any white Europeans had claimed it as theirs. A bloody civil war ensued. During that time The Salvation Army, equally vulnerable to attack, had to abandon some of its most useful mission hospitals and posts. Two white Salvationist workers at the Army's Usher school were murdered by rebel troops. In addition to the great tragedy of these two young women's lives, hundreds of black Zimbabwean Salvationists became victims of the conflict. Their loss would be duplicated in Uganda, South Africa, Mozambique, Kenya, Tanzania, and other places in Africa. The Army there has been a suffering Army, its subsequent rapid growth watered by the blood of thousands of martyrs.

The Salvation Army had never faced such widespread persecution, but Salvationists believed that the Army's mission would be advanced despite the suffering. The emerging world was teaching the Army that it not only would suffer but its mission would be blocked as well. Grappling with the new realities and developing new strategies formed the Army's major focus following the war.

Hearts Grown Cold

Other forces came into play as well. While Europe's economy was being resurrected, the scarred landscape repaired and new buildings erected, a growing cynicism replaced the faith of days gone by. There had been evidence of this prior to the war but now indifference and outright hostility to the Christian faith were expressed openly and without shame. In addition, a growing narcissism and secularism exalted the individual as supreme. The overriding concern in Western society was that the self be gratified. The result was a lowering of morals, an insatiable appetite of self–indulgence, an abandonment of concepts like honor and commitment. The Salvation Army was not exempt from these influences.

European membership statistics tell the tale. The number of officers fell from 11,432 in 1950 to 5,479 in 2003. The latter figure includes 2,640 retired officers, over 48 percent of the total. At the same time in Europe, the number of corps and outposts dropped from 4,927 to 2,471, a loss of close to 50 percent. Large Army forces in Norway, Sweden, and Great Britain skew these numbers, but there were losses across the board. Even now Scandinavia and Great Britain face critical personnel shortages, and things are likely to get worse before they get better. Statistics in *The Salvation Army Year Book* (2003) show that in Sweden retired officers outnumber active officers by a 3:2 ratio; in Norway there are slightly more retired officers than active, while in the United Kingdom territory 46 percent of the officers are retired.[11] The tremendous emphasis on missionary service in Europe over the years should be considered. Europe has contributed a disproportionate number of reinforcements to the Army's work in developing countries, and continues to supply a larger percentage of its officer personnel than any other region in the world. Thus the return of personnel available to carry on the work in their native lands has been diminished.

The territories of the United Kingdom, Sweden and Latvia, and Norway, Iceland, and the Faeroes still boast a very strong Army. The United Kingdom has 823 corps, outposts, and societies.[12] This is one for every 73,000 people compared with the United States with one center for every 178,500.

In Sweden the numbers are even better. With 328 corps and outposts, there is one for every 27,000 people. The Army in Sweden is the ninth largest Protestant denomination.[13] Norway, Iceland, and the Faeroes yield the most encouraging figures. With 834 corps and outposts in a total population of 4.5 million in Norway and another 280,000 in Iceland, the Army has one center for every 5,700 people.[14] Here the Army is the fifth largest denomination.

However, there has been little success in efforts to recruit new officers. In the United Kingdom territory in 2003 there were ninety–four cadets, seven in Norway, and three in Sweden.[15] But all is not bleak in Europe. Reopening of the work in Russia, Czech Republic, Hungary, and Latvia shows great promise for the future.

Down Under

Other Western nations have been similarly challenged, although not to the degree seen in Europe. Although geographically closer to Asia, Australia and New Zealand are culturally Western. The same factors that have injured the work in Europe have affected these two countries as well. During the same period as noted above, Australia (East and South) and New Zealand have fared much better than their European cousins, with a loss in the total officer force of less than 10 percent. However, 892 corps and outposts closed, a loss of over 63 percent.

North America

North America showed very mixed patterns for this period. Of Canada's 1,220 corps and outposts in 1950, 858 were lost by 2003, a staggering drop of 70 percent.[16] The officer force of 1,499 in 1950 grew to 1,925 by 2003, an increase of over 28 percent. This strengthening of officer personnel was consistent with what was happening in the United States as well, a surprising development given the similar cultural patterns of self–absorption found in Europe.

The four United States territories (Central, East, South, and West) reflect a net increase of 436 officers between 1950 and 2003. The number of corps and outposts increased slightly—a net gain of sixteen additional corps in over fifty years. Compared to Europe, Australia, and New Zealand, a much smaller proportion of Americans have served as reinforcement officers in developing countries. What is not possible to show is the tremendous growth in financial stability over the latter half of the twentieth century. Although operations struggled financially, the overall condition of the Army in the United States had improved dramatically. As a result, the international Army depended even more on the United States for its financial support than for its personnel.

Because of the tremendous media exposure and globalization of the world's market, there is a particular danger in peoples of a culture to view themselves as defining the entire world's experience. This phenomenon, called ethnocentrism, has led to grave misunderstandings and even to war.

But The Salvation Army experience has transcended any single culture. While the Army may have found itself struggling in some parts of the world, it prospered in others. The most profound shift following World War II had to do with the numeric strength of the Army.

Asia

The first non–Western field of Army service was established on the Indian subcontinent before the subsequent partitioning following independence and the political tensions in the region. Sri Lanka (Ceylon) was also an early field of work opened very soon after India. Although Christianity has always represented a tiny minority, the Army experienced good success in South Asia, where 20 percent of Salvation Army soldiers can be found. Because of their emerging status and religious minority commonalities, India, Pakistan, Bangladesh, and Sri Lanka will be considered together.

In 2003, the region had 3,779 officers, a 10 percent increase from 3,441 in 1950. The number of corps and outposts decreased from 5,946 to 4,433 (a 25 percent decline), a trend that continued until 1990 when new growth cancelled out some of the earlier losses. Some factors contributing to the declines may include the struggling economies of these countries and the decided minority status of Christianity in the region. Ethnic violence and the increasing militancy of indigent religions have also hampered the Army's work. A long civil war not only scarred Sri Lanka but severely affected the work in that country where independence did not bring prosperity.

Tightened immigration laws have made it increasingly difficult for reinforcement officers to serve in these countries, resulting in a shift to national officers. Although numerically the picture may appear bleak, in actual fact, India has gained by elevating national officers to positions of leadership. One of the Army's oldest fields of work will come to maturity through national process, conditions having forced Salvation Army strategy. India still remains a strong field for Army endeavor, with an encouraging upturn in strength over the past decade.

The rest of Asia presents a mixed picture. For example, there has been strong expansion in Korea. From fifty–two corps in 1950, the territory grew to 248 in 2003, an explosion of 478 percent. It doesn't appear that this growth is slowing in the least.

Japan, however, has suffered reverses. The Army's work shows a net gain of 20 percent (from fifty corps in 1950 to sixty in 2003) but in between it peaked to over 100 corps. Here again The Salvation Army seems to be subject to outside forces. Korea is fast becoming a Christian nation while Japan is deeply grounded in the Shinto religion augmented by an extremely materialistic culture.

The Army is showing encouraging growth in Indonesia, moderate growth in Hong Kong and the Philippines, while only negligible gains in Taiwan, Malaysia, and Singapore have occurred. These areas have also been subject to disruption by Islamic extremists and outright aggression. In addition, the Asian cultures in general view themselves as superior to Western ones. This is understandable in that the civilizations of Asia often predate any signs of organized culture or civilization in most of the rest of the world. In that Christianity has continued to be associated with Western societies, it faces an additional hurdle because of the culture. It is hoped that as Christianity continues to advance, the Army will grow stronger as well.

Latin America

Latin America and the Caribbean, where Christianity has long been the primary religion, present a very different picture. Though dominated by the Roman Catholic Church, strong expressions of animism, voodoo, and other folk religions remain. These at times have been blended with Christian beliefs to form a strange hybrid.

The Caribbean Territory, representing eleven nations, is the most diverse in the Army world. Not a single one could be considered prosperous, while Haiti ranks as one of the poorest in the world. Army work in Haiti has essentially leveled off. From 1950 to 2003 there was only a small increase in the number of officers (6 percent) while the number of corps increased by one. The poverty that marks the life of Salvation Army officers has made it difficult to retain promising young leaders. Although the economies are not strong in most of these island nations, other fields of endeavor are more lucrative than Salvation Army officership. For the less committed this has powerful sway.[17]

In Latin America, where the influence of the Roman Catholic Church has presented the Army some of its greatest challenges, the landscape changes. In particular, the Army's stance on the sacraments is problematic, and the Army is often viewed as a cult rather than a legitimate expression of Christianity.

Growth has continued, but it has been slow. As historic ties between the Catholic Church and various national governments unravel, the Army, along with other Protestant movements, has been given more opportunity to flourish.

The work in Brazil has struggled since the Army opened its work in this country with the largest Catholic population in the Western hemisphere. In eighty years, only fifty–five corps have been established, with 158 officers serving in the country. The past political instability of the country coupled with severe economic difficulties have taken their toll. Poverty and greed have contributed to the decimation of the Amazon rain forest, resulting in booming cities and impoverished shantytowns existing side by side.

In Spanish–speaking South America there are similar themes. In South America East, labor unions have infiltrated the Army, exacerbating efforts to deal with other critical problems. Once the strongest Army presence in Latin America, the territory has stagnated.

During Chile's communist rule, the Army suffered severe limitations, but with the advent of democracy the Army in South America West has begun to flourish. From thirty–five corps in 1950, the territory had grown by 275 percent to ninety–six corps by 2003. A corresponding growth of 53 percent in the officer corps has been realized for the same period. Most of the strength remains in Chile.

Latin America North, another territory composed of multiple nations, also shows encouraging signs of growth. Tiny Costa Rica, with a population of only 3.4 million, has become a model of Salvation Army operations for Latin America. The Army has grown steadily over 30 years and now has one center for every 283,000 people. The Salvation Army has been successful in maintaining close and friendly relations with the government, allowing for great freedom of operation. The high level of commitment of its officers and soldiers continues to fuel its evangelistic outreach.

Growing strength in this region led to a decision to realign the territory. Mexico became a separate command in 1998, and has since been elevated to the status of a territory. The rest of the Latin America North remained except for the addition of Spanish–speaking Cuba from the Caribbean Territory.

Although traditionally a difficult field of operations for the Army, Latin America overall has shown steady and consistent growth. A higher proportion of officers to cadets exists, a good sign for future expansion. A weakness in the work is noted by the fact that there have been only a few national leaders who have served as territorial commanders in any of the Latin American territories in the century–plus of Army operations. It is hoped that emerging leaders will change this regrettable situation.

The Promise of Africa

Once called the Dark Continent, Africa provides the brightest reasons to rejoice. A great chaos was created by the sudden disintegration of colonial governments following the Second World War. Government posts, including key positions in industries such as energy, transportation, mining and manufacturing, were dominated by expatriates from the colonial powers. The limited government participation national leaders were given failed to prepare the people to rule themselves. When the colonial powers left, a great vacuum was created. Without the opportunity to develop their leadership and administrative skills, the African people resorted to tribal loyalties, with tragic results. Arbitrary boundaries drawn between nations, regardless of local tribal ownership, produced disastrous results. It is still true that many Africans are far more loyal to their ancestral tribes than to the nations in which they are citizens.

The scourge of HIV/AIDS has also crippled development in Africa. At epidemic levels, the disease is killing a whole generation. Children are not exempt by any means, and many are born HIV positive and/or are orphaned when their parents succumb to the disease. Yet the continent remains one of vast resources and almost unlimited potential. It is hoped that Africa will get its own house in order so that it can assume its rightful place in world affairs. Recently, encouraging signs indicate that this may indeed be happening.

The Army in Africa faces problems of clashing cultures and religions. Although Christianity is making fantastic inroads, the Muslims are also moving aggressively in sub–Saharan Africa. If the religious differences were handled on a strictly ideological level it would be one thing but violence and intimidation are too often the forces used. Indigenous ancient faiths, including animism and witchcraft, and the village *shaman* remain influential in many villages and townships. It is not enough to dismiss these expressions as mere superstition; the people have been indoctrinated to believe in the power attributed to them.

Despite challenges, The Salvation Army has marched to a quickening pace. Exuberant Salvationism is attracting thousands to the Lord and the Army. Only limited economic resources keep the Army from a more rapid expansion—not that this seems to be holding anyone back. Indeed, the advance could be even more pronounced if economics did not limit the number of cadets that could be trained at any one time.

No clearer example of Army advance can be found than in the East Africa territory. East Africa has grown from 307 corps in 1950 to 1,761 corps and outposts in 2003—an astounding explosion of just under 575 percent—the largest number of soldiers of any territory in the world. The officer numbers are almost as impressive with an increase of 150 percent.[18] This is all the more compelling when one remembers that in 1950 there were far more expatriate officers than there were in 2003.

To the south, the Zimbabwe territory provides another example of African expansion. Despite losses in both personnel and facilities following a bloody and protracted civil war in the early 1970s, the Army rose from the ashes like the mythical phoenix. From 247 corps and outposts in 1950 to 792 in 2003, the territory has netted a 320 percent increase. One corps, society or outpost exists for every 14,000 people.

It is difficult to trace the progress of other African territories for this time period because territorial lines shifted after Africa was divided into twelve territories and commands from the five that existed in 1950. However, evidence of the overall growth can still be seen. In 1950 there were a total of 1,589 corps, outposts, and societies in all of Africa; in 2003 there were 4,387—an increase of 2,798—an incredible 175 percent increase. Clearly, the lay leadership of Africa has provided the impetus for much of the growth. While officer forces more than doubled, the many corps, outpost, and society openings did not keep pace. The expansion of The Salvation Army in Africa is not the result of consultation with church growth experts, nor does it reflect a push from headquarters. Rather, people have caught the vision of winning Africa for Christ.

While South Africa remains the most developed and prosperous country in sub–Saharan Africa, it has not enjoyed the same growth rate. It suffered greatly during the international boycott prompted by government apartheid policies. The boycott crippled the once–booming economy leaving internal turmoil that the nation is even now trying to correct. Southern Africa has shown a net gain of only two corps in the years 1950 to 2003, but realized an increase of 6 percent in its officer forces. In recent years the work in Mozambique has opened following its long civil war. Work there progresses slowly largely because the country's infrastructure was left in ruins with an economy to match. These statistics fail to show the huge losses sustained, but the territory has turned around and is now getting in step with the rest of Africa.

The Most Difficult Passage

The picture of the Army overall in the period following World War II is a mixed one. While there were huge gains in some areas of the world, losses were staggering in others. Comparing the figures from 1950 to 2003, The Salvation Army internationally declined in the number of its centers of worship from 16,847 to 15,456, a loss of 8.5 percent. The number of officers (including active and retired, auxiliary–captains, lieutenants, and envoys) increased by 5 percent.

The Army appears to enjoy the greatest progress among the emerging peoples of the world where its message of hope, salvation and practical service strike a responsive chord. The Army first took root among such people, and—in concert with William Booth's original vision—it is to these people that the Army still has the greatest appeal. The Salvation Army's chief threat comes not from outside opposition or dilution of its doctrines, but rather from the economic prosperity of its people.

The period following World War II has been the most difficult to face, but the Army's victories are no less glorious than the ones in its storied past. Successful warfare continued, but the defeats exacted a greater cost, and the Army's ability to recover was less rapid than in the past days. Like the weak and feeble among the children of Israel, who were attacked by the Amorites, much of the Army's loss has been sustained on the periphery where struggling corps were closed and where they were forced to retreat from hard places.

Denying the difficulty of these years will not help the Army. What will help is encouraging and advancing the fields and embracing the changes that must come. The world will not let the Army go back to a simpler time. While tradition gives the Army its sense of identity and continuity, it alone cannot define tomorrow. Whether in new fields today or in the old ones of East London, the Army's best strategy is innovation.

Having said that, the Army advances are strongest where local Army traditions are reinforced. Clamoring for change for the sake of change is as useless as clinging to the forms and monuments that have lost their meaning. The Army's unique culture is not something that should be denied or eliminated but it must be flexible.

The discouraging detail listed above is history and not current fact, and that is good news indeed. Indications are that the Army is stronger as it enters a new turning point.

Renewal

Perhaps the greatest symbol of the world's post–war distress was the Berlin Wall. Following the Second World War, Germany and its capital, Berlin, were partitioned by the occupying forces of France, Britain, the United States, and the Soviet Union. France, Britain, and the United States soon relinquished their sections but the Soviet Union maintained control over those allotted to them. This resulted in the division into two independent nations—West Germany and the Soviet satellite state of East Germany. Berlin was similarly partitioned and along the same lines reconstituted, except for East Berlin, which remained under Soviet control. Complicating the situation was the city's location, deep within the area controlled by East Germany.

As postwar tensions rose during the Cold War era, the East Germans erected a wall dividing their section of Berlin from the section operated by the government of West Germany. Because people seeking freedom were fleeing from the East to the West in such alarming numbers, the government elected to build the infamous Berlin Wall, which became a symbol of the animosity between the communist and non–communist world. Over the years, at least 80 people were killed by East German border guards as they attempted to escape to West Germany. Over 2.7 million people fled East Germany over the years, half of them through West Berlin.[1]

But cracks in the communist system began to show through the decade of the 1980s. It wasn't long until its façade lifted. After threatening world domination for the generation after World War II, communism itself was in full retreat. The world watched in amazement on November 9, 1989, as citizens of East Berlin began to demolish sections of the wall. It was the death knell of European communism. Guards stood by as in a matter of hours the wall that symbolized the worse in international relationships crumbled. A new era had begun.

A major shift in the international scene followed. The Soviet Union divided itself along ancient boundaries, creating independent states throughout Europe. The change was to have profound effect not only on the former communist nations but throughout the world. As often happens in international politics, monumental changes in one sphere resound far and wide.

Quickly seizing the initiative, General Eva Burrows worked to reintroduce The Salvation Army to Russia. Driven from there in 1918 following the communist takeover of that country, the opening of the work in Russia represented far more than the opening of work in a new country, as significant as that is in itself. The opening of the work in that country was a significant victory. It represented the Army's retaking ground it had lost and reclaiming a vision that had been badly damaged by the decades that followed. This event signaled a change. It reawakened the core purpose deep in the genetic code of the Salvationist. Despite its many accompanying problems, marching into Russia in a very real sense was reclaiming the future from the past.

The Salvation Army's commitment to bring the world to Christ was renewed. Doctrinal justification for such themes as postmillennialism was unnecessary. The opportunities were real and present, and the people were in need. They began turning their lives over to the Lord, and the Army is growing as a result. In the truest sense, the Army has never found itself better equipped, educated, or well known. Worldwide, its officer and soldier strength has never been greater. This is the time for the Army to move forward. The rediscovery of its core purpose of bringing the world to Christ has been the single greatest indicator of the Army's change of direction, as stated by John Larsson in his first article to officers following his election as General:

> I believe that The Salvation Army is going through a time of the most remarkable process of renewal. The Holy Spirit inspired process of renewal has been happening worldwide—with what has been taking place at an international level being a reflection of what has been happening in territories, divisions and corps. . . . It is therefore a good time to be a Salvationist! We are part of a dynamic process. And if in this process of renewal, we as an Army succeed in recapturing our passion for mission and develop a new self–understanding of the unique contribution we are meant to make, even greater things await the Army in the future.[2]

The process of renewal has been defined by pain and possibility, and it is not finished. It would be foolish to say with any certainty what will happen, or how the Army will look and act a generation from now. However, forces are at work and issues are being addressed that may indicate how the Army will be shaped.

Before attempting to outline these, it should be noted that they are by no means universal. A burning issue in France may have little relevance in Indonesia. It is a mistake for a culture to assume that it represents the thinking of the entire human race. If anything is seen on the horizon it is not a world consensus but a sharpening of differences between cultures. The Salvation Army will not escape this challenge any more than any other institution.

The Army overall is responding well to the challenges. To be sure, there are those who feel the old ship turns too slowly, but one of the Army's great strengths has been its ability to adapt but not abandon. A man who tries to live at seventy as he did at seventeen will prove himself a fool and likely suffer for it. He must adapt to life changes that inevitably come. In doing so, however, he does not abandon the lessons learned at seventeen or purge his memory because he is in a different stage of life. In the same way, The Salvation Army must continue its balance between adapting to new realities, while not abandoning its roots or too readily casting aside its traditions.

Many of the factors determining The Salvation Army's future are not new issues at all. Outside of Scripture, there are no once–and–for–all answers. Every generation must affirm the validity of the issues it faces. By way of example, it is not enough for a new soldier to assent to abstinence from alcohol because the Army says so. He must accept that standard for himself and be strengthened by the Army stance. It will never be enough that William Booth responded to the lostness of his world unless the coming generation responds to the lostness of its world. His dedication, however wonderful it might be, is only a bit of nineteenth century history unless it serves as a beacon to the soul who chooses to live his life for the same great purpose.

What are the dynamics that direct the Army now as it enters its third century?

Decline in Western Influence

A perceptible decline in Western influence is apparent around the world. At the turn of the century the dominance of Britain as a world power was unquestioned. It is not so today. Britain has had to unite with other European nations, not so much to extend an empire but to secure mutual help and protection. Although the United States continues as a world power, its influence is clearly declining as well, as evidenced by its increasing inability to engender cooperation on international issues. Its dominance in manufacturing has been challenged by nations whose populations are willing to produce goods for fewer dollars. Secularization has weakened the moral influence of the West as it seeks to find answers outside traditional Christian values.

This worldwide vacuum has given rise to Asian and Islamic influence. Of the seven largest economies, four belong to non–Western nations: Japan (second), China (third), Russia (sixth), and India (seventh).[3] With the world still largely dependent on Middle East oil, the Islamic states are likely to continue to strengthen economically. This is particularly troublesome given the anti–Christian leanings of many of these states.

These factors create critical implications for The Salvation Army. Its economic lifeblood is still found within the Western nations. As the twenty–first century progresses and the economic balance continues to move to other parts of the world, Salvation Army work requiring Western funds for support will be impacted. In these emerging economies the Army has not yet fully succeeded in making itself a valuable social force worthy of widespread public support. Cultures that see suffering as the punishment for sin committed in a previous life will have a hard time with the Army's worldview. To interfere would be to interrupt the person's progress to a higher plane.

Amid a tightening world economy, International Headquarters funds for world projects have begun to dry up in recent years, slowing the growth of exciting potential fields such as Eastern Europe, Africa, and Asia. Even if the economies of the emerging nations show dramatic improvement, it is not clear that the level of expertise exists within the Army to capitalize on that prosperity. Also, it cannot be assumed that fundraising methods successful in the West will work elsewhere. The Army already operates on a no–frills basis in most of the world. Cutting back in many places can only mean curtailing vital work.

Women and the World

The Army was a pioneer in giving women equal access in its structure, but this stance is not so remarkable anymore. In government, business and the Church, women continue to demonstrate their ability to lead. This is remarkable, given the perspective of history, even though progress in women's equality may not be satisfactory to many. The status of women in countries where women are kept in a subservient role is not that much different from that of women a century ago in Christian cultures.

The vision as outlined by William and Catherine Booth, in which women continue to emerge as leaders in all walks of life, has not yet been achieved. In North America, only one territory is led by a woman (Commissioner M. Christine MacMillan in Canada), and since 1880, none of the four United States territories can claim more than three women divisional commanders in all of their history. Although the record is much better internationally, it has been limited at best. Women continue to be underrepresented in proportion to their numbers on international and territorial commissions and boards. Only single men have fared worse overall.

Yet there is again a call for a stronger role for women. The clearest signal was given by General Paul Rader when he declared in Minute 1995/1A/13 in May, 1995, that married women officers would carry rank in their own names rather than their husband's, that they would receive their own appointments, and that their years of service would be recognized in determining promotion to the next rank. This has changed the way some appointments are made. For example, it is now more likely that a married woman officer will have a corps appointment in the same area in which her husband serves on a headquarters. In some divisions women now have a command role, while the husband serves in a supporting role.

The issue was addressed by the Commission on Officership. Its final report stated:

> Women officers, single and married, represent a significant and strategic part of officer ministry worldwide.

> It is recognized that the effective service of women officers is vital to the mission of the Army.

> A number of women officers experience frustration and lack of fulfillment, perceiving that they are not considered for certain appointments due to gender or marital status.

All women officers, married or single, should be considered for all appointments according to their ability.

It is recognized that consultation will need to take place, particularly in relation to separate appointments for married couples.

Recommendation: We recommend that all territories affirm the ministry of women officers by appointing them to positions commensurate with their gifts and experience.

Recommendation: We recommend that territories seek a gender balance in the membership of planning and decision–making bodies.

Organizational Changes

Changes in Salvation Army government also signal the new millennium as a turning point. The Salvation Army Act of 1980 set in motion the mechanism to separate International Headquarters from the British territory (now called the United Kingdom territory). This was akin to separating conjoined twins, so intertwined were the operations of the two theoretically separate commands.

The separation has been a particular boon to the United Kingdom. Much of the finances and an excessively large proportion of the personnel for International Headquarters had been furnished by the British field. While this provided a great sense of continuity for International Headquarters, it did not reflect the Army's internationalism. For its part, Great Britain did not have control over its own finances as the priorities of International Headquarters often superceded those of the country. Even while the territory was suffering a decline in personnel, it furnished large numbers of officers for the international Army.[4]

For International Headquarters, the transition has been more challenging. While it has the ability to access officers from across the Army world, not all can adapt to the change in culture represented by life in the United Kingdom. Although a largely British staff kept IHQ from a truly global focus, the officers at least were accustomed to life in London. IHQ has been challenged financially with the loss of income from national appeals and legacies. The adjustment appears in the IHQ building itself. A major refurbishing will convert half the building into rental spaces, helping to underwrite its operating costs.

The separation has advantages as well. Although no mention of any such plan has been made, IHQ is no longer bound to be located in Great Britain. If circumstances dictated, it could be relocated to Geneva or some other city. Limited access to the British field may actually mean that IHQ will become something of a Salvation Army United Nations. This will undoubtedly affect leadership and development decisions in parts of the world previously under–represented.[5]

Further indications of organizational change were reflected in the convening of the Commission on Officership in October 1998. Reviewing nearly all aspects of officership, the international commission explored how to open officership to more individuals and to make it more flexible, while keeping the overall mission of the Army intact.

Renewal and Advance

For the forty years between 1950 and 1990 the Army as a whole not only reached a plateau but actually declined. That decrease has finally ended, and an encouraging upward swing is noted. The 1995 and the 2003 editions of *The Salvation Army Year Book* indicate that the number of corps has grown from 14,907 to 15,456, an increase of over 3 percent. A 26.6 percent increase in soldiers from 797,910 to 1,010,829 was also noted, as well as a rise in officers and auxiliary captains. These increases are all the more important given the short span of time represented. It is interesting to note that although the numbers are more dramatic in some parts of the world, comparisons show that the increases are almost universal. They hardly represent a movement that is winding down; rather, they indicate an Army on an aggressive march.

Although regarded as a traditionally Western product, The Salvation Army is considerably less white than in years past. In total numbers of soldiers, eight out of the top ten territories are non–white. Of the two primarily white territories, USA South is showing its greatest numerical advances among African–Americans and Hispanics.[6]

Although the numbers continue to shift in favor of non–white territories, top Army leadership continues to be dominated by Europeans or those of European descent. This tendency has more to do with opportunity than disenfranchisement. Top leaders tend to come from countries that offer educational and administrative opportunities, which are severely limited in emerging nations. But as these emerging nations tackle literacy problems and become more proficient in business development, the long–range outlook of the Army's leadership and staffing regimen is likely to be very different indeed.

Leadership Development

As mentioned earlier, many territories in the world have been in existence for as long as 100 years but have not yet placed a national officer in charge. As a variety of world governments move to restrict entry of non–citizens and insist on national leadership, the Army could face great difficulty.

At the 1998 International Conference of Leaders, former Chief of the Staff Commissioner Earle A. Maxwell outlined "five essential qualities/ qualifications necessary for Salvation Army leadership . . . spiritual authority, relational skills, management skills, diverse experience and education, global perspective and vision."[7] It is essential that potential leaders be identified and prepared to carry out the mission of the Army.

The Information Age

The proliferation of computers, fax machines, the Internet, and the resulting explosion of knowledge is changing the way the Army communicates. Websites dispense both international and local information daily that relate to Army activities and positions. Long–term changes are difficult to predict, but ease of communication between far–flung places can only be an advantage as ties between Salvationists are strengthened by contact. On the other hand, the increasing reliance on these modes of communication may result in increased isolation as faxes replace phone calls and emails replace visits. There is no substitute for personal contact and the sharing of mutual experiences.

The evidence is undeniable. The Army of today and the coming one of tomorrow are decidedly different than the Army of even twenty years ago.

What Does It All Mean?

When William and Catherine Booth walked the streets of East London, they could not have imagined what God would do with their vision and labor. Many suppose he would look at the modern–day Army with disdain. I think otherwise. The Army of Booth's day was fraught with problems, and there were unworthy people in the ranks then. They experienced overstretched supply lines and shortages of personnel, but opportunities to test God's faithfulness were plentiful.

I believe that most Salvationists have a fierce loyalty to their Lord and a burden for a decaying world around them. The Founders, who fought desperately to save people from poverty and pain might be concerned over ominous creaking of the old ship, but they would see that it is moving unmistakably ahead. It was never a perfect vessel, but it was one that William and Catherine Booth envisioned, and continued to build even as it was being sailed. It remains so for us.

"God didn't need another church in the world," General Wilfred Kitching once said, "but He did need a Salvation Army." The challenge remains for the Army to be the tool the Lord can use to save a lost world.

Endnotes

Turning Point One

1. Booth–Tucker, *Catherine Booth: Mother of The Salvation Army*, p. 83.
2. Kew, *Catherine Booth: Her Continuing Relevance*, p. 2.
3. Prescott, *The Salvation Army: The Secret of Its Success*, p. 85.
4. Stead, *Catherine Booth*, p. 91.
5. Bramwell–Booth, *Catherine Booth: The Story of Her Loves*, p. 50.
6. Kew, *Catherine Booth*, p. 3.
7. Bramwell–Booth, *Catherine Booth*, p. 181.
8. Booth, *Papers on Practical Religion*, p. 157.
9. Booth, *The Highway of Our God*, p. 94.
10. Bramwell–Booth, *Catherine Booth*, p. 186.
11. Railton, *Heathen England*, pp. 120–22.
12. Ibid., p. 94.
13. Booth, *Echoes and Memories*, pp. 168–69.
14. Quoted in Sandall, *The History of The Salvation Army*, Vol. 1, p. 215.
15. Prescott, *The Salvation Army*, p. 80.
16. March 16, 1886.
17. Booth, *The Founder's Messages to Soldiers*, pp. 188–89.
18. "International Commission on Officership, Final Report."
19. In *The Officer*, September/October 2003, p. 33.
20. Quoted in Larsson, *My Best Men Are Women*, p. 83.
21. Booth, *Founder's Messages*, p. 176.
22. In *Staff Review*, Vol. VI–B, pp. 298–99.
23. Booth, *Founder's Messages*, p. 192.

Turning Point Two

1. Collier, *The General Next to God*, p. 26.
2. Ervine, *God's Soldier: General William Booth*, p. 386.
3. Sandall, *History*, Vol. 1, p. 188.
4. Horridge, *The Salvation Army: Its Origin and Early Days*, p. 30.
5. Sandall, *History*, Vol. 1, p. 189.
6. Ibid., p. 198.
7. Ervine, *God's Soldier*, p. 387.
8. Redstone, *An Ex–Captain's Experience of The Salvation Army*, p. x.
9. Bailey, *Search Light on Salvation Army Government*, p. 12.
10. Britnell, *The New Papacy*, p. 11.
11. Prescott, *The Salvation Army*, pp. 94–95.
12. Manson, *The Salvation Army and the Public: A Religious, Social and Financial Study*, p. 199.
13. *The Salvation Army Year Book*, 1916.
14. Quoted in Begbie, *The Life of General William Booth: The Founder of The Salvation Army*, Vol. 1, pp. 411–14.
15. Collins and Porras, *Built to Last*, p. 9.

Turning Point Three

1. Horridge, *The Salvation Army*, p. 34.
2. Begbie, *The Life*, p. 405.
3. *The Salvation Army Year Book*, 1948.
4. *Salvationist*, September 1878, p. 225
5. Christian Mission Pamphlet, 1878.
6. Sandall, *History*, Vol. 1, p. 231.
7. *Salvationist*, February 1879, p. 29.
8. Booth, *Echoes and Memories*, p. 66.
9. Begbie, *The Life*, pp. 410–11.
10. Sandall, *History*, Vol. 2, p. 42.
11. Ervine, *God's Soldier*, p. 449.
12. Quoted in Horridge, *The Salvation Army*, p. 46.
13. Gariepy, *Mobilized for God: The History of The Salvation Army*, Vol. 8, p. 87.
14. Baird, *The Banner of Love*, pp. 7–8.
15. *The Song Book of The Salvation Army*, 1987, #681.
16. Ibid., #593.
17. Sandall, *History*, Vol. 2, p. 113.
18. Collins and Porras, *Built to Last*, p. 71.
19. *Orders and Regulations for The Salvation Army*, 1878, p. 9.
20. Manson, *The Salvation Army and the Public*, p. 221.
21. *The Salvation War: 1882*.
22. *Pall Mall Gazette*, N.D.
23. Sandall, *History*, Vol. 2, pp. 151–52.
24. Quoted in Horridge, *The Salvation Army*, p. 115.
25. *Wilson Carlile and the Church Army*, p. 66.
26. *Salvationist*, October 10, 1998, p. 7.
27. Collins, *Good to Great*, p. 141.

Turning Point Four

1. Sandall, *History*, Vol. 4, p. 208.
2. Bullard, *A Missionary's Memories*, p. 7.
3. Murdoch, *Origin of The Salvation Army*, p. 136.
4. *Fighting in Many Lands*, p. 11.
5. Gariepy, *Mobilized for God*, Vol. 8, p. 88.
6. Huntington, *The Clash of Civilizations: The Remaking of the World Order*, p. 70.
7. Orsborn, *The House of My Pilgrimage*, p. 141.
8. Gariepy, *Mobilized for God*, Vol. 8, p. 107.
9. Correspondence with Stephen Court, November 13, 1997.

Turning Point Five

1. Rightmire, "Samuel Brengle and the Development of Salvation Army Pneumatology," *Word & Deed*, Fall 1998, p. 41.
2. Horridge, *The Salvation Army*, p. 116.
3. Booth, *Echoes and Memories*, p. 191.
4. Quoted in Green, *Catherine Booth: A Biography of the Cofounder of The Salvation Army*, p. 164.

5. Ervine, *God's Soldier,* p. 464.

6. Green, *Catherine Booth,* p. 237.

7. Rightmire, "Samuel Brengle and the Development of the Salvation Army Pneumatology," *Wesleyan Theological Journal,* Spring–Fall, 1992, p. 118.

8. Booth, *Echoes and Memories,* p. 192.

9. Booth, *Popular Christianity,* pp. 42–43.

10. Tuck, *Saints Without Sacraments,* p. 8.

11. Booth, *Echoes and Memories,* p. 193.

12. Ibid.

13. Begbie, *The Life,* Vol. 1, p. 425.

14. Ibid., p. 432.

15. Ervine, *God's Soldier,* p. 472.

16. Begbie, *The Life,* Vol. 1, pp. 424–25.

17. Booth, *Echoes and Memories,* p. 193.

18. *War Cry* (London), January 13, 1883, p. 4.

19. Quoted in Hope, *Mildred Duff: A Surrendered Life,* p. 178.

20. Sandall, *History* Vol. 2, pp. 132–33.

21. Ibid.

22. Begbie, *The Life,* Vol. 1, p. 433.

23. Lunn, *Review of the Churches,* April 1895.

24. *War Cry* (London), January 17, 1883.

25. Cunningham, in *The Staff Review,* May 1929, p. 163.

26. General Orders for Special Services, p. 5.

27. Quoted in Rightmire, pp. 93–94.

28. *Called to Be God's People.*

29. Gariepy, *Mobilized for God,* Vol. 8, pp. 85–86.

30. Needham, *Community in Mission,* p. 8.

Turning Point Six

1. Booth, *In Darkest England and the Way Out,* p. 59.

2. Booth, *Echoes and Memories,* pp. 118–20.

3. Unsworth, *Maiden Tribute: A Study In Voluntary Social Service,* p. 28.

4. Quoted in Hope, *Mildred Duff,* p. 30.

5. Ibid., pp. 29–30.

6. Quoted in Coutts, *Bread for My Neighbor,* pp. 52–53.

7. Coutts, *Bread for My Neighbor,* p. 55.

8. Sandall, *History,* Vol. 3, p. 36.

9. Murdoch, *Origin of The Salvation Army,* p. 154.

10. Booth, *In Darkest England,* p. 28.

11. Horridge, *The Salvation Army,* p. 10.

12. Tuchman, *The Proud Tower,* p. 73

13. Booth, *In Darkest England,* p. 18.

14. Sowerby in *All the World,* December 1890, p. 652.

15. Booth, *In Darkest England,* pp. xviii–xxi.

16. *All the World,* August 1890, p. 356.

17. Booth, *In Darkest England,* p. 25.

18. Ibid., p. 27.

19. Ibid., p. 55.

20. Ibid., p. 81.

21. Ibid., p. 53.

22. Ibid., p. 71.

23. Ibid., pp. 100–101.

24. Thompson in *The Salvation Army Year Book*, 1941, p. 23.

25. *Atlanta Constitution,* December 10, 1890.

26. Nicol, *General Booth and The Salvation Army*, p. 208.

27. Coates, *Prophet of the Poor*, p. 243.

28. Booth, International Congress Addresses 1904, Booth, p.26.

Turning Point Seven

1. Tuchman, *The Proud Tower*, p. 270.

2. Ecksteins, *Rites of Spring: the Great War and the Birth of the Modern Age*, p. 129.

3. Ibid., p. 100.

4. Johnson, *Modern Times: The World from the Twenties to the Nineties*, p. 48.

5. Ibid., pp. 6–9.

6. Purviance, "War Talk," SA USA National Archives, 20.68.

7. SA USA National Archives Correspondence, 20.117.

8. SA USA National Archives Correspondence, 20.15.

9. Background information on songs furnished by Taylor, *Companion to the Song Book.*

10. McKinley, *Marching to Glory*, p. 93.

11. *The War Cry* (USA), January 12, 1895, p. 4.

12. Information furnished by International Heritage Centre.

Turning Point Eight

1. Nicol, *General Booth and The Salvation Army*, pp. 110–11.

2. Smith, *The Betrayal of Bramwell Booth*, p. 254.

3. Unpublished article by Gunpei Yamamuro for *The Staff Review*, 1929.

4. Smith, *Betrayal*, p. 28.

5. *The War Cry*, December 27, 1879, p. 4.

6. Horridge, *The Salvation Army*, p. 89.

7. Court Document, January 17, 1929.

8. McKinley, *Marching to Glory*, p. 194.

9. Tuchman, *The Proud Tower*, p. 9.

10. Johnson, *Modern Times*, p. 18.

11. Quoted in Sandall, *History,* Vol. 1, p. 167.

12. Mackenzie, *The Clash of the Cymbals: The Secret History of the Revolt in The Salvation Army*, pp. 37–38.

13. Smith, *The Betrayal of Bramwell Booth*, p. 42.

14. Tuchman, *The Proud Tower*, p. 16.

15. Mackenzie, *The Clash of the Cymbals*, p. 40.

16. Correspondence of Commander Evangeline Booth to Mrs. General Florence Booth 10/27/25, International Heritage Centre Archives.

17. Mackenzie, *The Clash of the Cymbals*, p. 63.

18. Booth, "Black Friday Interview with the General," July 23–24, 1920, International Heritage Centre Archives.

19. Carpenter correspondence 10/28/28, International Heritage Centre Archives.

20. Murdoch, *Origin of The Salvation Army*, p. 126.

21. McKinley, *Marching to Glory: The History of The Salvation Army in the*

United States, 1880–1992, p. 195.

22. Correspondence from Edward Higgins to Evangeline Booth, 6/8/23, International Heritage Centre Archives.

23. Mackenzie, *The Clash of the Cymbals*, p. 72.

24. Satterlee, *Sweeping Through the Land*, pp. 124–25.

25. Correspondence from Evangeline Booth to Mrs. General Florence Booth, 10/27/25, International Heritage Centre Archives.

26. Correspondence from Evangeline Booth to Frederick Booth–Tucker, 5/31/25, International Heritage Centre Archives.

27. Correspondence from Minnie Carpenter to Mary Booth, 10/29/28, International Heritage Centre Archives.

28. Correspondence from Evangeline Booth to Bramwell Booth, 2/9/28, International Heritage Centre Archives.

29. Correspondence from Evangeline Booth to Bramwell Booth, 2/24/28; Isaac Unsworth to Evangeline Booth 3/25/28; William Peart to John McMillan, 6/7/28; Evangeline Booth to Frederick Booth–Tucker, 6/13/28, International Heritage Centre Archives.

30. Mrs. Booth's reply, p. 15, International Heritage Centre Archives.

31. Ibid., p. 16.

32. Frost, quoted in unnamed newspaper account, 1/24/30.

33. Correspondence from Commissioner Whatmore to Florence Booth, 9/21/28; Commissioner Jeffries to Evangeline Booth, 10/30/28; Commissioner William Peart to Commissioner Mapp, 11/19/28; Commissioner Jeffries to Lt. Colonel Albert Orsborn, 12/27/28; Court Document 1/17/29, International Heritage Centre Archives.

34. Batchelor, *Catherine Bramwell–Booth*, p. 184.

35. Court Document, 1/17/29; Mrs. Booth's Reply, p. 21, International Heritage Centre Archives.

36. Notes by Evangeline Booth in copy of Mrs. Booth's reply, p. 25, SA USA National Archives.

37. Mrs. Booth's Reply, p. 21, International Heritage Centre Archives.

38. Correspondence from William Peart to Jeffries, 6/15/28, International Heritage Centre Archives.

39. Mrs. Booth's Reply, pp. 24–27, International Heritage Centre Archives.

40. Correspondence from William Peart to unknown addressee, 9/19/28, SA USA National Archives.

41. Correspondence from Commissioner Jeffries to Evangeline Booth, 10/30/28, SA USA National Archives.

42. Mrs. Booth's Reply, pp. 29–30; Correspondence from Commissioner Cunningham to Commissioner Hay, 11/2/28, International Heritage Centre Archives.

43. Correspondence from William Frost to Edward Higgins, 12/28, International Heritage Centre Archives.

44. Mrs. Booth's Reply, p. 35, International Heritage Centre Archives.

45. "'Power from on High' or 'Power from Below,'" 1/29, International Heritage Centre Archives.

46. Correspondence from Samuel Logan Brengle to Jeffries, 1/14/29, SA USA National Archives.

47. Correspondence from Bramwell Booth to members of the High Council, 1/14/29, International Heritage Centre Archives.

48. Correspondence from Samuel Logan Brengle to Jenkins, 1/14/29, SA

USA National Archives.

49. Correspondence from Edward Higgins to High Council, 1/19/29, International Heritage Centre Archives.

50. Correspondence from Evangeline Booth to Jenkins, 1/23/29, SA USA National Archives.

51. *John Bull*, 1/26/29.

52. Damon diaries, 3/1/1929, SA USA National Archives. Used by permission.

53. *The War Cry*, 1/22/30.

54. Unpublished manuscript for *The Staff Review*, p. 173, International Heritage Centre Archives.

Turning Point Nine

1. Johnson, *Modern Times*, p. 370.

2. Coutts, *The History of The Salvation Army*, Vol. 7, p. 17.

3. Ibid., p. 123.

4. Ibid., p. 21.

5. Ibid., p. 60.

6. Ibid., p. 22.

7. Ibid., p. 54.

8. Ibid., pp. 52–53.

9. Ibid., p. 52.

10. Ibid., p. 41.

11. Information taken from *The Salvation Army Year Book*, 1950 & 1985. It is very important to note that this information is at least two years behind the publication date. In reality, the published 1950 figures are for 1948, the 1985 figures for 1983.

12. *The Salvation Army Year Book,* 2003.

13. Ibid., p. 518.

14. Ibid., pp. 271, 428.

15. *The Salvation Army Year Book*, 2003.

16. The loss included both corps and outposts but the vast majority of these closings were outposts. It is assumed that some operations were consolidated and that other less efficient ones were closed. But even taking outposts out of the picture, the territory has sustained a large decrease.

17. Interviews with Commissioners, March 1998.

18. *The Salvation Army Year Book*, 1950, 1995.

Turning Point Ten

1. "Berlin Wall," Microsoft® Encarta® Online Encyclopedia 2003 http://encarta.msn.com © 1997–2003 Microsoft Corporation. All Rights Reserved.

2. "Renewal," *The Officer*, November–December 2002.

3. Huntington, *The Clash of Civilizations: Remaking of World Order*, p. 87.

4. International Commission on Officership: The Salvation Army.

5. Interview with Commissioner Dinsdale Pender; Interviews with Commissioner Dinsdale Pender, Commissioners James Osborne, Orval Taylor, David Baxendale, Albert and Frances Scott, Willard Evans, Colonels Leon Ferraez, Wallace Conrath, Lt. Colonels Leon Turner, Donald and Audrey Seiler.

6. Ibid.

7. *The Salvation Army Year Book,* 1998.

8. *The Officer,* August 1998, p. 6.

Bibliography

Books

Bailey, R. *Search Light on Salvation Army Government,* London: Christian Literature Depot, 1902.

Baird, Catherine. *The Banner of Love,* London: Salvationist Publishing and Supplies, n.p.

Batchelor, Mary. *Catherine Bramwell–Booth,* Tring, England: Lion Publishing, 1986.

Begbie, Harold. *The Life of General William Booth: The Founder of The Salvation Army,* 2 vols. New York: Macmillan Company, 1920.

Booth, Bramwell. *Echoes and Memories,* New York: George H. Doren Company, 1925.

Booth, Catherine. *The Highway of Our God,* London: Salvationist Publishing and Supplies, 1954.

———. *Papers on Practical Religion,* London: The Salvation Army, 1891.

Booth, William. *The Founder's Messages to Soldiers,* London: The Salvation Army Book Department, 1921.

———. *International Congress Addresses,* London: The Salvation Army Book Department, 1904.

———. *In Darkest England and the Way Out,* Atlanta: The Salvation Army, 1890.

Booth–Tucker, Frederick. *Catherine Booth: Mother of The Salvation Army,* London: The Salvation Army Book Department, 1910.

Bramwell–Booth, Catherine. *Catherine Booth: The Story of Her Loves,* London: Hodder and Stoughton, 1970.

Britnell, Albert. *The New Papacy,* Toronto: n.p., 1889.

Coates, T. F. G. *Prophet of the Poor,* London: Hodder and Stoughton, 1905.

Collier, Richard. *The General Next to God: The Story of William Booth and The Salvation Army,* London: Fontana/Collins, 1965.

Collins, James C. and Jerry I. Porras. *Built to Last,* New York: Harper Collins Publishers, 1994.

Collins, Jim. *Good to Great,* New York: Harper Business, 2001.

Coutts, Frederick. *Bread for My Neighbour,* London: Hodder and Stoughton, 1978.

———. *The History of The Salvation Army,* Vol. 7, London: Hodder and Stoughton, 1986.

Covenant Services, London: The Salvation Army Book Department, 1906.

Ecksteins, Morris. *Rites of Spring: The Great War and the Birth of the Modern Age,* New York: Anchor Books, 1989.

Ervine, St. John. *God's Soldier: General William Booth,* New York: Macmillan, 1935.

Fairbank, Jenty. *Booth's Boots: Social Work Beginnings in The Salvation Army,* London: The Salvation Army, 1983.

Fighting in Many Lands, Third Series. London: The Salvation Army, 1960.

Gariepy, Henry. *Mobilized for God: The History of The Salvation Army, Volume 8: 1977–1994,* Atlanta: The Salvation Army, 1999.

Green, Roger J. *Catherine Booth: A Biography of the Cofounder of The Salvation Army,* Grand Rapids: Baker Books, 1996.

Harris, Wesley. *Battle Lines,* Toronto: The Salvation Army, 1992.

Hope, Noel. *Mildred Duff: A Surrendered Life,* London: Salvationist Publishing and Supplies, 1935.

Horridge, Glenn. *The Salvation Army: Its Origin and Early Days,* Godalming, England: Ammonite Books, 1993.

Huntington, Samuel P. *The Clash of Civilizations: The Remaking of World Order,* New York: Touchstone, 1997.

"International Commission on Officership, Final Report," London: The Salvation Army International Headquarters, 2000.

Johnson, Paul. *Modern Times: The World from the Twenties to the Nineties,* New York: Harper Collins Publishers, 1992.

Johnstone, Patrick and Jason Mandryk. *Operation World: When We Pray God Works,* Carlisle, Cumbria, UK: Campus Crusade Asia Ltd., 2001.

Kew, Clifford W. *Catherine Booth: Her Continuing Relevance,* London: The Salvation Army, 1990.

Larsson, Flora. *My Best Men Are Women,* New York: The Salvation Army, 1974.

Mackenzie, F. A. *The Clash of the Cymbals: The Secret History of the Revolt in The Salvation Army,* New York: Brentano's, 1929.

Manson, John. *The Salvation Army and the Public: A Religious, Social and Financial Study,* London: George Routledge & Sons Ltd., 1906.

McKinley, Edward H. *Marching to Glory: The History of The Salvation Army in the United States, 1880–1992,* Grand Rapids: William B. Eerdmans Publishing Co., 1995.

Murdoch, Norman. *Origin of The Salvation Army,* Knoxville: University of Tennessee Press, 1994.

Needham, Philip D. *Community in Mission: A Salvationist Ecclesiology,* Atlanta: The Salvation Army, 1987.

Nicol, Alex. *General Booth and The Salvation Army,* 1910.

Noll, Mark A. *Turning Points: Decisive Moments in the History of Christianity,* Grand Rapids: Baker Books, 1997.

Orsborn, Albert. *The House of My Pilgrimage,* London: Salvationist Publishing and Supplies, 1958.

Prescott, P. *The Salvation Army: The Secret of Its Success,* London: Christian Commonwealth Publishing Co., Ltd., 1891.

Railton, George Scott. *Heathen England*, London: SW Partridge and Co., 1879.

Redstone, J. J. R. *An Ex–Captain's Experience of The Salvation Army*, 1888.

The Salvation Army Year Book, London: The Salvation Army (1915, 1950, 1955, 1960, 1965, 1970, 1975, 1980, 1985, 1990, 1995, 1998).

The Salvation War 1882, London: The Salvation Army, 1883.

Sandall, Robert. *The History of The Salvation Army*, Vol. 1. New York: Thomas Nelson and Sons, Ltd., 1947.

———. *The History of The Salvation Army*, Vol. 2. London: The Salvation Army, 1950.

———. *The History of The Salvation Army*, Vol. 3. London: Thomas Nelson and Sons, Ltd., 1955.

Satterlee, Allen. *Notable Quotables: A Compendium of Gems from Salvation Army Literature*, Atlanta: The Salvation Army, 1985.

———. *Sweeping Through the Land: The History of The Salvation Army in the Southern United States*, Atlanta: The Salvation Army, 1988.

Smith, Frank. *The Betrayal of Bramwell Booth*, London: Jarrolds Publishers, 1929.

The Song Book of The Salvation Army, New York: The Salvation Army, 1997.

Stead, W. T. *Catherine Booth*, London: James Nisbet and Co., 1900.

Taylor, Gordon. *Companion to the Song Book*, Atlanta: The Salvation Army, 1990.

Tuchman, Barbara W. *The Proud Tower*, New York: Ballantine Books, 1996.

Tuck, Brian. *Saints Without Sacraments*, Johannesburg: The Salvation Army, 1997.

Unsworth, Madge. *Maiden Tribute: A Study in Voluntary Social Service*, London: Salvationist Publishing and Supplies, 1954.

Watson, Bernard. *A Hundred Years' War*, London: Hodder and Stoughton, 1964.

Wiggins, Arch R. *The History of The Salvation Army*, Vol. 4, London: Thomas Nelson and Sons, Ltd., 1964.

Wilson Carlile and the Church Army, London: The Church Army Book Room, 1926.

Articles

Bramwell–Booth, Catherine. "Are the Women to Blame?" *Staff Review* [London] (1926).

Larsson, John. "Renewal." *The Officer* [London] (2002).

Maxwell, Earle. "Address to the International Conference of Leaders." *Officer* [London] (1998).

Sowerby, Commissioner. "A Review of 'In Darkest England.'" *All the World* (1890): 652.

"The World in 1995." *War Cry* (1895)

Crest Books

The Salvation Army National Publications

Crest Books, a division of The Salvation Army's National Publications department, was established in 1997 so contemporary Salvationist voices could be captured and bound in enduring form for future generations, to serve as witnesses to the continuing force and mission of the Army.

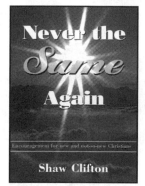

Never the Same Again
Encouragement for new and not–so–new Christians
by Shaw Clifton

This book explains the fundamentals and deeper aspects of faith in down–to–earth language, offering great encouragement and sound instruction. Whether readers are new Christians or revisiting the foundations of faith, the author helps them see that as they grow in Christ, they are *Never the Same Again*. An ideal gift for new converts.

Christmas Through the Years
A War Cry *Treasury*

Along with kettles and carols, the *Christmas War Cry* remains one of The Salvation Army's most enduring yuletide traditions. The anthology contains classics that have inspired *War Cry* readers over the past half century. Longtime subscribers will find this treasury to spark their memories, while those new to *The War Cry* will benefit from a rich literary heritage that continues to the present day.

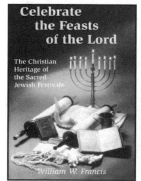

Celebrate the Feasts of the Lord
The Christian Heritage of the Sacred Jewish Festivals
by William W. Francis

This critically acclaimed book offers a fresh perspective on the sacred Jewish festivals, revealing their relevance to modern–day Christians. The work describes how Jesus participated in the feasts and how, in Himself, their meaning was fulfilled. Study questions at the end of each chapter make this book perfect for group or individual study.

Pictures from the Word
by Marlene J. Chase

This collection of 56 meditations brings to life the vivid metaphors of Scripture, addressing the frequent references to the vulnerability of man met by God's limitless and gracious provision. The author's writing illustrates passages often so familiar that their hidden meaning eludes us. *Pictures from the Word* will enrich your time of personal devotion and deepen your understanding of the Word.

A Little Greatness
by Joe Noland

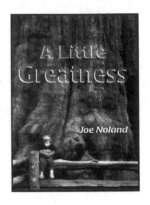

Under the expert tutelage of auhor Joe Noland, readers explore the book of Acts, revealing the paradoxes of the life of a believer. Using word play and alliteration, Noland draws us into the story of the early Church while demonstrating the contemporary relevance of all that took place. A Bible study and discussion guide for each chapter allow us to apply each lesson, making this an ideal group study resource.

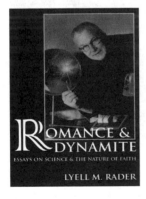

Romance & Dynamite
Essays on Science and the Nature of Faith
by Lyell M. Rader

"Whatever God makes works, and works to perfection. So does His plan for transforming anyone's life from a rat race to a rapture." Anecdotes and insights on the interplay between science and faith are found in this collection of essays by an "Order of the Founder" recipient known as one of The Salvation Army's most indefatigable evangelists.

Who Are These Salvationists?
An Analysis for the 21st Century
by Shaw Clifton

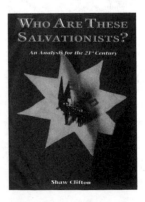

A seminal study that explores The Salvation Army's roots, theology, and position in the body of believers, this book provides a definitive profile of the Army as an "authentic expression of classical Christianity." Salvationists and non–Salvationists alike will find this to be an illuminating look at the theology which drives the social action of its soldiers.

Easter Through the Years
A War Cry *Treasury*

This Easter, spend time reflecting on the wonderful gift of salvation God has given by reading *Easter Through the Years,* a companion volume to *Christmas Through the Years.* Articles, fiction, poetry, and artwork culled from the last fifty years of the *Easter War Cry* will recount the passion of Christ and unveil the events surrounding the cross and the numerous ways Easter intersects with life and faith today.

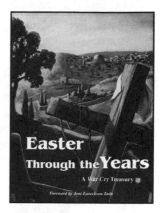

He Who Laughed First
Delighting in a Holy God
by Phil Needham

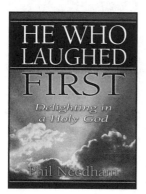

This invigorating book questions why there are so many sour–faced saints when the Christian life is meant to be joyful. Needham explores the secret to enduring joy, found by letting God make us holy to become who we are in Christ—saints. *He Who Laughed First* helps the reader discover the why and how of becoming a joyful, hilarious saint.

Slightly Off Center!
Growth Principles to Thaw Frozen Paradigms
by Terry Camsey

Church health expert Terry Camsey seeks to thaw frozen paradigms of what is "Army." Challenging us to see things from a different perspective, he urges his readers to welcome a new generation of Salvationists whose methods may be different but whose hearts are wholly God's—and whose mission remains consistent with the principles William Booth established.

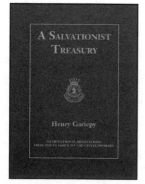

A Salvationist Treasury
365 Devotional Meditations from the Classics to the Contemporary
edited by Henry Gariepy

This book brings to readers the devotional writings from over a century of Salvationists. From Army notables to the virtually unknown, from the classics to the contemporary, this treasure trove of 365 inspirational readings will enrich your life, and is certain to become a milestone compilation of Army literature.

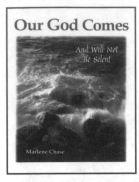

Our God Comes
And Will Not Be Silent
by Marlene J. Chase

Like the unstoppable ocean tide, God reveals Himself throughout all creation and will not be silent. The author shares in her poems the symmetry in all creation that draws us toward the goodness of God. She invites the reader to distinguish His voice that speaks as only our God can speak.

Fractured Parables
And Other Tales to Lighten the Heart and Quicken the Spirit
by A. Kenneth Wilson

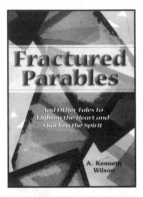

By applying truths of Scripture to contemporary situations, we find that people of the Bible are as real as we are today. Wilson illuminates beloved biblical accounts in a new light by recasting Jesus' parables in modern circumstances and language. He challenges as he entertains us, helping readers see the humor in the mundane while deftly showing the spiritual application.

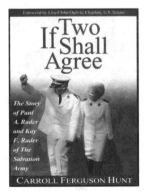

If Two Shall Agree
The Story of Paul A. Rader and Kay F. Rader of The Salvation Army
by Carroll Ferguson Hunt

The author tells the fascinating story of how God brought these two dedicated servants together and melded them into a compelling team who served for over 35 years, leading the Army to new heights of vision, ministry, and growth. Read how God leads surrendered believers to accomplish great things for Him.

Pen of Flame
The Life and Poetry of Catherine Baird
by John C. Izzard with Henry Gariepy

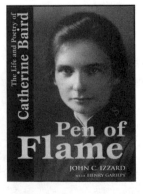

Catherine Baird lived a life of extraordinary artistic value to The Salvation Army. As a poet, hymn writer, and editor, Baird changed the way the Army viewed the importance of the written word. From a decade of research and devotion John C. Izzard has painted a compelling word picture of one of the Army's strongest and yet most delicate authors.

Andy Miller
A Legend and a Legacy
by Henry Gariepy

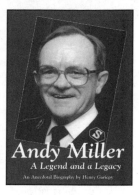

As an American Salvationist, Andy Miller has had a powerful spiritual impact on innumerable lives, both within and outside the ranks of The Salvation Army. His vast ministry across the nation has left its indelible impact upon countless people. Through anecdotes, this biography conveys the story of one of the most colorful and remarkable leaders in the Army's history.

A Word in Season
A Collection of Short Stories

"For every season of our lives," writes Lt. Colonel Marlene Chase in her introduction, "the world of story can help us define our experience and move us beyond ourselves." More than thirty writers, including Max Lucado, have contributed to this compilation, which features factual accounts as well as fictional narratives within the panoply of Christian belief. It's the everyday experiences made extraordinary through faith.

Sanctified Sanity
The Life and Teaching of Samuel Logan Brengle
by R. David Rightmire

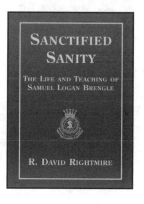

Many Salvationists may still recognize the name, but fewer appreciate the influence that Brengle had on the development of the Army's holiness theology. Dr. Rightmire has written a theological reassessment of Brengle's life and thought to reacquaint those of the Wesleyan–holiness tradition in general, and The Salvation Army in particular, with the legacy of this holiness apostle.

Leadership on the Axis of Change
by Chick Yuill

In great demand as a conference and retreat speaker, Major Yuill describes today's Christian church as an institution that "faces great challenges stemming from inert cynicism within and dynamic changes without." Part manual on the functions and principles of leadership, part declaration of the need for change, this book serves all spiritual leaders with both provocation to action and direction toward success.

Living Portraits Speaking Still
A Collection of Bible Studies

Employing the art of compilation, Crest Books draws on established officer authors and contributors to *The War Cry* to examine the brilliance and vulnerabilities of the "saints of Scripture." *Living Portraits Speaking Still* groups eighteen Bible studies by theme, as a curator might display an artist's paintings. Each "gallery" focuses on a different aspect of God: Portraits of Sovereignty, Provision, Perfection, Redemption, and Holiness.

The First Dysfunctional Family
A Modern Guide to the Book of Genesis

Bible families are just like ours—loving, caring, and as out of control and dysfunctional. In tracing the generations from Creation, Major A. Kenneth Wilson shows us how we may avoid our ancestors' mistakes in our family relationships. And through all of this dysfunctional rebellion, reconciliation, and return, readers will see that God is there, never giving up on us despite how badly we have treated Him and each other.

All titles by Crest Books can be purchased through your nearest Salvation Army Supplies and Purchasing department:

ATLANTA, GA—(800) 786–7372
DES PLAINES, IL—(847) 294–2012
RANCHO PALOS VERDES, CA—(800) 937–8896
WEST NYACK, NY—(888) 488–4882